A WORDSWORTH COLOUR GUIDE

HELICOPTERS

Wordsworth Editions

First published in England 1993 by
Wordsworth Editions Ltd
Cumberland House
Crib Street
Ware
Hertfordshire SG12 9ET

Copyright © 1993 by Aldino Ltd
147 Cleveland Street, London W1P 5PH, England

ISBN 1 85326 803 8

The editors and publishers have pleasure in
thanking the helicopter manufacturers throughout
the world, without whose assistance
this book would not have been possible, and particular
for their generous response with photographs.

Cover: Sikorsky SH-60B Sea Hawk
Opposite: a glimpse of the future: McDonnell Douglas
Canard Rotor/Wing (CRW) conceptualisation

Produced by Aldino Limited
Text conversion and pagination by
August Filmsetting, St Helens, UK
Printed and bound in Italy by Amadeus S.p.A.

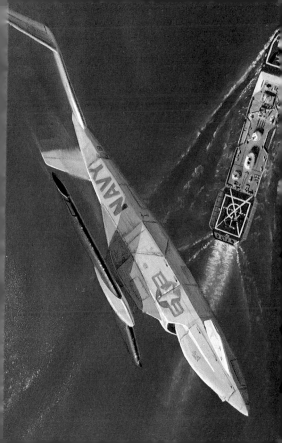

Contents

State-of-the-art development in digital avionics integration, advanced airfoils and rotorcraft aerodynamics and advances in composite-materials fabrication and manufacturing techniques are incorporated in the Boeing 360 Advanced Technology demonstrator. This is the world's largest all- composite helicopter, and one of the fastest, having achieved speeds of 397km/h (246mph) in level flight. Ongoing tests should justify applications of these advanced technologies to other programs

European Helicopter Industries EH 101
Merlin is the UK Royal Navy's new
6 *ASW helicopter; 44 have been ordered*

US Army Sikorsky UH-60A Black
8   Hawks

*A Westland Sea King on exhibition,
the British license-built version of
the Sikorsky S-61*

10

Introduction

Two independently-built helicopters succeeded in getting their wheels off the ground in France as early as 1907, but the likes of Dorand, Flettner and Focke needed another 30 years before developing machines which actually flew.

Their story only really began in 1939, when Igor Sikorsky, a Russian emigré, with great determination coaxed his VS-300 into flight. His vision was always of a lifesaving function, and early craft were generally those which today we should describe as search and rescue (SAR).

It was Flettner who provided the first helicopter to enter combat service, but this, like the Focke-Achgeles of 1944, is an almost-forgotten step in the history of aviation. Today's remarkably versatile and powerful helicopters continue to save lives, in addition to their potent fighting capabilities. Able to perform vital functions over both battlefields and oceans, their capabilities have grown to match the diversity of the missions that they fly; anti-tank and ground attack, scouting and reconnaissance, heavy transport, SAR, anti-submarine, airborne and early warning, command and control. The technology continues to develop as the number of helicopters in both military and civil service increases almost daily.

Success! The first flight, on 14 September 1939, of the VS-300 with Igor Sikorsky at the controls

Conversion table

1 Imp gal = 4.561 litres
1 US gal = 3.7853 litres
1km = 0.621 mile
1 kW = 1.34hp
1 litre = 2.201 US pints/1.761 Imp pint
1m = 3.281ft/1.0936 yards
1m^3 = 35.315 cu ft
1mm = 0.0394in
1 tonne = 1,000kg/2,205lb

The main rotor-head assembly of the UH-60A Black Hawk. The system consists of a titanium hub assembly and four articulated blades with titanium spars and fiberglass skins. Elastomeric bearings replace conventional roller element bearings in the hub, and eliminate bearing maintenance. A bifilar vibration absorber consisting of four masses is tuned to lower vibration at the hub, which in turn reduces vibration throughout the airframe.

Aérospatiale SA 319B Alouette III

Country of origin: France
First flight: 1957
Type: light utility/communications
Crew/accommodation: one, and six passengers
Powerplant: one 589kW (789shp) Turboméca Astazou XIV turboshaft
Dimensions: rotor diameter 11.02m (36ft 1.8in); length with rotors turning 12.84m (42ft 1.5in)
Weights: empty 1,090kg (2,403lb); max take-off weight 2,205kg (4,960lb)
Max speed: 220km/h (136mph) at sea level
Range: 605km (375 miles) with six passengers
Armament: variants can carry up to 500kg (1,102lb) of ordnance, which can include two lightweight anti submarine torpedoes
History: the Alouette III was developed in the late 1950s as an improvement to the Alouette II, with larger cabin and improved equipment, all-round performance and greater power. About 1,350 were produced in two basic versions at four plants in France, India, Romania and Switzerland. The SA 316B was powered by the 425kW (570shp) Artouste IIIB turboshaft, and the SA 319B is detailed above.

The Alouette III is a classic helicopter and undertook a wide range of roles from air-taxi and mountain rescue to
anti-submarine and observation

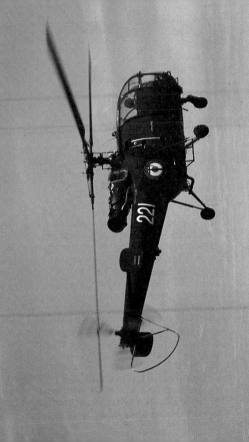

Aérospatiale SA 321H Super Frelon

Country of origin: France
First flight: 7 December 1982
Type: medium assault and tactical transport
Crew/accommodation: two, and up to 30 troops
Powerplant: three 1,170kW (1,570shp) Turboméca Turmo IIIE6 turboshafts
Dimensions: rotor diameter 18.9m (62ft); length with rotors turning 23.03m (75ft 6.7in)
Max take-off weight: 13,000kg (28,660lb)
Cruising speed: 248km/h (154mph) at sea level
Operational range: 814km (506 miles)
Payload: 5,000kg (11,023lb) freight carried either internally or externally
History: developed from the smaller S.A. 320 Frelon, with the help of Sikorsky, who designed the rotors; it first entered service in the above form as a troop carrier. Variants include the SA 321G naval model, SA 321J civil model and Israeli SA 321K, which uses General Electric T58 turboshafts, and the SA 321L and J military models, developed for Libya, South Africa and China, which now builds the type as the Harbin Z-8.

The Super Frelon was originally powered by three 985kW (1,320shp) Turmo IIIC2 turboshafts, but entered service with the revised powerplant detailed above

18

Aerospatiale SA 321G Super Frelon

Country of origin: France
First flight: 3 December 1982 as the SA 321H
Type: search and rescue
Crew/accommodation: three or four, and 27 survivors or 15 litters plus two attendants
Powerplant: three 1,156kW (1,550shp) Turboméca Turmo IIIC6 turboshafts
Dimensions: rotor diameter 18.9m (62ft); length with rotors turning 23.03m (75ft 6.7in)
Max take-off weight: 13,000kg (28,660lb)
Max speed: 275km/h (171mph) at sea level
Operational range: 1,019km (633 miles)
Payload: 5,000kg (11,023lb) freight
History: the SA 321G variant operated by the French Navy is differentiated from the other variants by its stabilizing floats of fuselage fairings and is deployed primarily in the protection of the approaches to the nuclear submarine base at Brest. It has a secondary SAR tasking, for which it is equipped with Sylphe search radar and a 276kg (606lb) capacity winch, located in the starboard door with 90m (295ft) cable.

The naval Super Frelons have stabilizing floats and an air-opening rear ramp/door that facilitates the launching of bulky rescue items such as inflatable rafts

Aérospatiale Puma HC.Mk 1

Country of origin: France/UK
First flight: July 1968 (British-built)
Type: tactical transport
Crew/accommodation: two, and 16 soldiers
Powerplant: two 984kW (1,320shp) Turboméca Turmo IIIC4 turboshafts
Dimensions: rotor diameter 15m (49ft 2.5in), fuselage length 14.1m (46ft 1.5in)
Max take-off weight: 6,400kg (14,110lb)
Max speed: 286km/h (174mph) at sea level
Operational range: 629km (391 miles)
Armament: provision for anti-tank missiles, rockets, fixed cannon or side-firing machine guns
History: designed as an all-weather tactical helicopter for the French Army, the Puma was originally planned with a single 1,417kW (1,900shp) Turboméca Bastan turboshaft, but prototypes appeared with the Turmo IIIs. In Spring 1968, the UK agreed to co-operate with France on a program of three new helicopters, including the Puma, and Westland built 40 SA 330E variants for the RAF, as the Puma HC.Mk 1, which entered service in 1972; also eight Puma SA 330L (standard Mk 1s with composite rotor blades, Turmo IVC turboshafts and particle separators in the inlets).

Aérospatiale's upgraded Super Puma

Aérospatiale SA 330L Puma

Country of origin: France
First flight: April 1965
Type: search and rescue
Crew/accommodation: three/four, and 16 survivors or six litters and six seated survivors
Powerplant: two 1,175kW (1,575shp) Turboméca Turmo IVC turboshafts
Dimensions: rotor diameter 15m (49ft 2.6in); length with rotors turning 18.2m (59ft 6.6in)
Max take-off weight: 7,500kg (16,535lb)
Max speed: 262km/h (163mph) at sea level)
Operational range: 550km (342 miles)
Payload: 3,000kg (6,614lb)
History: developed as a battlefield helicopter, capable of carrying 20 troops, the Puma has all of the necessary SAR features with all-weather flight capability and a reliable twin-engined powerplant. The type also features optional inlet de-icing and snow/ice shields. The winch has a capacity of 275kg (606lb) and has 90m (295ft) of cable. Most SAR variants have been fitted with Bendix RDR 1400 or RCA Primus 40/50 nose-mounted search radar

The Puma is ideal for its SAR role, combining good payload and performance with an all-weather flight capability. The Super Puma AS 332L2 illustrated is a straightforward upgrade of the 330

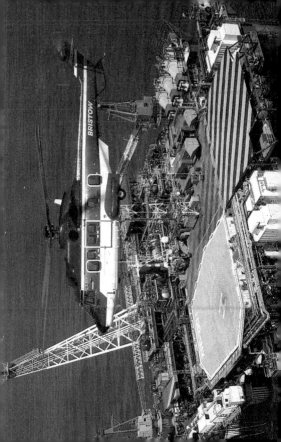

Aérospatiale AS 332L Super Puma

Country of origin: France
First flight: September 1977 (AS 331 prototype)
Type: medium-lift/general purpose transport
Crew/accommodation: two and 24 troops
Powerplant: two 1,324kW (1,725shp) Turboméca Makila 1A turboshafts
Dimensions: rotor diameter 15.08m (49ft 5.5in); length with rotors turning 18.73m (61ft 5.5in)
Max take-off weight: 8,350kg (18,410lb)
Cruising speed: 278km/h (173mph)
Operational range: 634km (394 miles)
Payload: 2,727kg (6,012lb) freight carried internally or 4,500kg (9,921lb) slung load
History: a straightforward upgrading of the SA 330 Puma with increased power, uprated transmission and a Starflex lightweight rotor head. The main rotor blades can be thermally de-iced and the Super Puma has much improved landing gear. Variants include the AS 332C with accommodation for 17, and the stretched AS 332L, with a 0.76m (2ft 5.9in) longer cabin seating 21, greater fuel capacity and an additional two windows. The latest Super Puma Mk II has a revised rotor, uprated gearbox and improved avionics; its military variant is the AS 532 U2 Cougar capable of carrying 29 commandoes.

Aérospatiale Gazelle HT.Mk 3

Country of origin: France
First flight: April 1967
Type: utility and training
Crew/accommodation: one, and up to four troops
Powerplant: one 44kW (590shp) Turboméca Astazou IIIA turboshaft
Dimensions: rotor diameter 10.5m (34ft 5.5in); fuselage length 9.53m (31ft 3.2in)
Max take-off weight: 1,800kg (3,968lb)
Max speed: 264km/h (164mph) at sea level
Hovering ceiling: 5,000m (16,400ft)
Operational radius: 669km (416 miles)
Armament: none
History: the SA 341 was designed to replace the Alouette II series of utility helicopters and was one of the three types covered in the Anglo-French co-production agreement of 1968. The main British AH.Mk 1 variant was produced by Westland for the British Army, although the Royal Navy HT.Mk 3 (training helicopter) and RAF HCC.Mk 4 (communications type) variants were produced in small numbers and these began to enter service from mid-1973.

The SA 341 Gazelle uses the same powerplant as the SA 318C Alouette II; however, the SA 342 variant uses the more powerful Astazou XIV

28

Aérospatiale AS 350B Ecureuil

Country of origin: France
First flight: April 1974
Type: light general purpose
Crew/accommodation: one, and five passengers
Powerplant: one 478kW (641shp) Turboméca Arriel turboshaft
Dimensions: rotor diameter 10.69m (35ft 0.75in); length with rotors turning 12.99m (40ft 7.5in)
Max take-off weight: 2,100kg (4,630lb)
Cruising speed: 232km/h (144mph)
Operational range: 700km (435 miles) at sea level
History: designed specifically for operation at low cost and low maintenance, with the added advantage of relatively low vibration and noise levels. The AS 350C and AS 350D Astar variants which are sold in North America use 459kW (616shp) Lycoming LTS 101 turboshafts. The AS 350 is also manufactured in Brazil, as the Helibras Esquilo. Another variant, the twin-engined AS 355, is sold in North America as the Twinstar and elsewhere as the Ecureuil 2, the largest version of which has a strengthened fuselage section and two 317kW (425shp) Allison 250-C20F turboshafts.

The latest AS 355F2 variant Ecureuil, an ideal transport helicopter for flight above cities and IFR flights

Aérospatiale SA 365C Dauphin 2

Country of origin: France
First flight: June 1972
Type: general purpose
Crew/accommodation: one, and nine passengers
Powerplant: two 492kW (660shp) Turboméca Arriel 1A turboshafts
Dimensions: rotor diameter 11.68m (38ft 4in); length with rotors turning 11.97m (39ft 3.25in)
Max take-off weight: 3,400kg (7,496lb)
Cruising speed: 254km/h (158mph) at sea level
Operational range: 465km (289 miles)
Payload: 1,360kg (2,998lb) freight carried internally or 1,300kg (2,866lb) slung load
History: the SA 360 was planned as a larger brother to the Ecureuil and originally flew powered by a single 730kW (980shp) Astazou XVI turboshaft. Variants include both civil and military models in both single and twin-engined versions. The SA 361 can carry 13 troops or operate in the anti-tank role with missile armament. The range includes the SA 365M Panther battlefield helicopter with TM333 turboshafts, the SA 365N naval version with anti-ship or anti-submarine sensors and weapons, and the civil SA 365C with retractable landing gear.

The SA 365N is also built in China at Harbin, with the designation Z-9.

Opposite is the AS 365N2 Dauphin

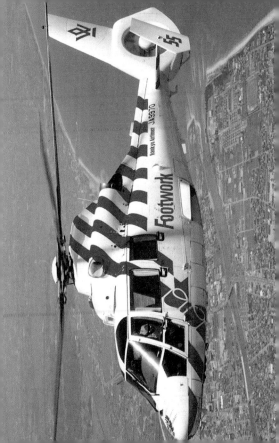

Aérospatiale SA 365F Dauphin 2

Country of origin: France
First flight: 1972
Type: search and rescue
Crew/accommodation: three crew
Powerplant: two 522kW (700shp) Turboméca Arrial 1M turboshafts
Dimensions: rotor diameter 11.00m (30ft 1.7in); length with rotors turning 13.46m (44ft 2in)
Max take-off weight: 4,100kg (9,039lb)
Max speed: 296km/h (184mph) at sea level
Operational range: 880km (547 miles)
Payload: eight survivors, or four litters plus an attendant or 1,600kg (3,527lb) of freight carried as an external underslung load
History: developed in a wide-ranging number of forms since the basic SA 360 civil type, the SA 365F can be fitted with Thomson-CSF ORB 32 Hercules II or Bendix RDR 1500 search radar, in addition to an autopilot and the Crouzet ONS 200A advanced navigation system. The rescue hoist is side-mounted, with 90m (295ft) of cable, rated at 275kg (606lb). US Coast Guards use the type HH-65A Dauphin (SA 366G-1), which is powered by 507kW (680shp) Avro Lycoming LTS 101-750A-1 turboshafts, and is equipped with a Northrop Sea Hawk FLIR sensor.

Originally designated the AS 365M, this upgraded military version became the AS 565 Panther

Agusta A109A Mk II

Country of origin: Italy
First flight: August 1971
Type: light general purpose
Crew/accommodation: two, and six troops
Powerplant: two 313kW (420shp) Allison 250-C20B turboshafts
Dimensions: rotor diameter 11m (36ft 1in); length with rotors turning 13.05m (42ft 9.75in)
Max take-off weight: 2,600kg (5,732lb)
Cruising speed: 266 km/h (165mph) at sea level
Hovering ceiling: 4,968m (16,300ft)
Operational range: 615km (382 miles)
Payload: passengers, internally-carried freight or 907kg (2,000lb) underslung load
History: owing to problems, the initial production Model A109A was not available until 1975. Originally planned with a single 514kW (690shp) Turboméca Astazou II turboshaft, Agusta recast the helicopter with a more reliable twin-turbo powerplant. Agusta began delivery of the uprated A109A Mk II in September 1981. This later version included several improvements such as a new tail rotor and engine mountings, to reduce vibration and noise.

The Agusta A109A Mk II Hirondu incorporated many operating improvements and retained its fully-retractable tricycle landing gear and sleek lines

36

Agusta-Bell AB.212 ASW

Country of origin: Italy/USA
First flight: October 1956, as the Bell 204
Type: search and rescue
Crew/accommodation: two or three seats
Powerplant: one 1,398kW (1,875shp) Pratt & Whitney Canada PT6T-6 Turbo Twin Pac
Dimensions: rotor diameter 14.63m (48ft); length with rotors turning 17.4m (57ft 1in)
Max take-off weight: 5,070kg (11,177lb)
Max speed: 185km/h (115mph) at sea level
Search range: 615km (382 miles)
Payload: seven survivors or four litters plus an attendant or 2,268kg (5,000lb) freight
History: Bell developed the 204 into the 205 with a larger cabin. A further development, to provide the Canadian Armed Forces with a medium-lift helicopter, produced the Model 212. The AB.212 is license-built in Italy for the Italian Air Force in the SAR role. The AB.212 ASW is operated by other air arms in the anti-submarine/ship role, with secondary SAR tasking. SAR instrumentation includes search radar with the antenna housed in a radome above the cockpit, advanced navigation systems, and an automatic flight control system. The rescue winch is on the starboard side, rated at 272kg (600lb).

A twin-engined variant of the Bell 205/UH-1H, built under license in
38 *Italy by Agusta*

Bell Model 47/UH-13H Sioux

Country of origin: USA
First flight: December 1945
Type: civil and military light utility
Crew/accommodation: one, and two passengers
Powerplant: one 194kW (260hp) Avro Lycoming TVO-435-AlA
Dimensions: rotor diameter 10.69m (35ft 9.5in); length with rotors turning 13.11m (43ft)
Max take-off weight: 710kg (1,564lb)
Cruising speed: 137km/h (85mph) at sea level
Hovering ceiling: 4,023m (13,200ft)
Operational range: 383km (238 miles)
Payload: 454kg (1,000lb) load, externally slung

History: the Bell Model 47 was the first helicopter in the world to achieve civil certification in March 1946. The model was built in a number of variants, including the classic Bell 47D, which featured the 'goldfish bowl' cockpit and the Bell 47G definitive production model. It was also built under license in Italy (Agusta-Bell) and in the UK (Westland), mostly as the Sioux AH.Mk 1 general-purpose helicopter for the Army Air Corps and for the RAF as the Mk 2 trainer, of which only 15 were built.

The Bell Model 47G-3B-4 variant was the one used by the RAF as a trainer at the Central Flying School's

Bell Model 205/UH-1H Iroquois

Country of origin: USA
First flight: entered service September 1967
Type: search and rescue
Crew/accommodation: two or three crew
Powerplant: one 1,044kW (1,400shp) Avro Lycoming T53-L-13
Dimensions: rotor diameter 14.63m (48ft); length with rotors turning 17.62m (57ft 9.7in)
Max take-off weight: 4,309kg (9,500lb)
Max speed: 204km/h (127mph) at sea level
Service ceiling: 3,840m (12,600ft)
Operational range: 512km (318 miles)
Payload: 14 survivors or six litters, plus one attendant or 1,759kg (3,880lb) freight
History: the Bell 205, developed from the Model 204 and known as the 'Huey' series, has been produced in the USA and under license in Italy, Japan, Taiwan and Germany. The variants are numerous, including the UH-1D/H military versions and short-range SAR. Although the 205 has an excellent flight record, it is without all weather flight instrumentation/search capabilities. The hoist is situated on the starboard side of the cabin, above the sliding door.

The Model 205 fulfilled a large variety of roles around the world, but was limited to clear-weather operations

Bell Model 206L-3 LongRanger III

Country of origin: USA
First flight: January 1966
Type: light general-purpose
Crew/accommodation: two, and five passengers
Powerplant: one 485kW (656shp) Allison 250-C30P turboshaft
Dimensions: rotor diameter 11.28m (37ft); length with rotors turning 13.02m (42ft 8.5in)
Max take-off weight: 1,882kg (4,150lb)
Cruising speed: 215km/h (134mph) at 1,524m (5,000ft)
Operational range: 635km (395 miles)
Payload: 750kg (1,650lb)
History: initially developed as a scout for the US Army the five-seat Bell Model 206 JetRanger became one of the world's most successful helicopters, entering service as the OH-58 Kiowa. This was developed into the OH-58D armed scout, with a mast-mounted sight and a varied armament capability. The basic 206 was developed for civil use as the Model 206L LongRanger with a longer cabin and a larger-diameter main motor, driven by a 313kW (420shp) 250-C20B turboshaft, which was upgraded for the LongRanger II and further upgraded for the LongRanger III, allowing greater payload and higher performance.

The OH-58A Kiowa, military
44   *forerunner of the 206L Long Ranger*

Bell Model 209/AH-1W Super Cobra

Country of origin: USA
First flight: 1980
Type: attack anti-armor
Crew/accommodation: two crew
Powerplant: two 1,212kW (1,625shp) General Electric T700-GL-401 turboshafts
Dimensions: rotor diameter 14.63m (48ft); overall length 17.68m (58ft)
Max weight: 6,900kg (4,285lb)
Max speed: 305km/h (190mph)
Operational range: 402km (250 miles)
Armament: three-barrelled M197 20mm (0.78in) gun in chin turret plus rocket pods, cluster weapons, Minigun, TOW or Hellfire anti-armor missiles
History: developed as an uprated Model 209 AH-1T, it was designed for the US Marines as an attack helicopter with much enhanced operational capability. Deliveries began in March 1986, and duties include troop carrying, escort, and anti-armor multiple weapon fire support.

The 209 AH-1 Hueycobra was developed to act as a gunship escort for UH-1 troop helicopters in Vietnam, with stub wings for disposable armament and a cannon mounted on the fuselage chin. This was further developed as outlined above for the US Marine Corps

Bell Model 212/UH-1N Iroquois

Country of origin: USA
First flight: 1968
Type: search and rescue
Crew/accommodation: two crew
Powerplant: one 962kW (1,290shp) Pratt & Whitney Canada T400-CP-400
Dimensions: rotor diameter 14.69m (48ft 2.25in); fuselage length 12.92m (42ft 4.75in)
Max take-off weight: 4,762kg (10,500lb)
Max speed: 228km/h (142mph) at sea level
Operational range: 400km (248 miles)
Payload: 12 survivors or 1,534kg (3,383lb) freight
History: widely used throughout the world in the SAR version, the Model 212 is an important helicopter in all its variants. A development of the Model 205, the 212 has a twin engined powerplant for increased all-round performance. It is also equipped with IFR, providing an all-weather capability, and with a standard US rescue hoist rated at 272kg (600lb). The latter is situated above the sliding cabin door on the starboard side.

Initially developed as the 204 for the US Army, it was altered to the UH-1 in 1962, and complemented by the larger-cabined 205 or UH-1D and later the UH-1H series. This, in turn, was partnered by the quite similar 212 (UH-1N)

Bell Model 214ST

Country of origin: USA
First flight: November 1977
Type: medium general purpose
Crew/accommodation: two, and 16 or 18 passengers
Powerplant: two 1,212kW (1,625shp) General Electric CT7-2A turboshafts
Dimensions: rotor diameter 15.85m (52ft); length with rotors turning 18.95m (62ft 2.25in)
Max take-off weight: 7,938kg (17,500lb)
Cruising speed: 250km/h (155mph) at 1,220m (4,000ft)
Operational range: 806km (501 miles)
Payload: 8.95m^3 (316cu ft) of freight, carried internally
History: the Bell Model 214ST (Super Transport) was developed from the UH-1H military variant and is essentially an upgraded Huey plus. Originally designated 'stretched Twin', it is a commercial variant with a strengthened structure and also a twin-turbine powerplant which provides greater reliability where deployed by resources-exploration companies for flights over water. Two variants are available, in 16 or 18-seat configurations.

Certificated for IFR flights, the 214ST with twin-turbine powerplant has proved to be exceptionally reliable since its introduction in 1977

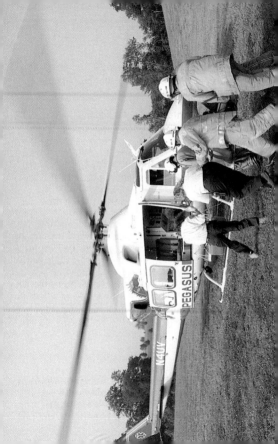

Bell Model 222B

Country of origin: USA
First flight: August 1976
Type: light commercial/executive transport
Crew/accommodation: one or two crew, and up to eight passengers
Powerplant: two 510kW (684shp) Lycoming LTS 101-750C-1 turboshafts
Dimensions: rotor diameter 12.8m (42ft); length with rotors turning 15.36m (50ft 4.8in)
Max take-off weight: 3,742kg (8,250lb)
Cruising speed: 259km/h (161mph)
Operational ceiling: 4,815m (15,800ft)
Operational range: 532km (330 miles)
Payload: up to 540kg (1,190lb)
History: the first North American-produced twin-turbine commercial helicopter, the Model 222 features retractable tricycle landing gear, low-vibration Noda-Matic cabin suspension, fiberglass/stainless steel main rotor blades and a no-lubrication elastomeric main rotor hub. The Model 222B has single-pilot IFR qualification without a stability-augmentation system.

The 222A initial model is available in both Executive and offshore configurations, with the single-piloted 222B being the latest variant

Bell Model 412SP

Country of origin: USA
First flight: August 1979
Type: high-performance utility
Crew/accommodation: one, and 14 passengers
Powerplant: two 671kW (900shp) Pratt & Whitney Canada PT0T-0D 1 turboshafts
Dimensions: rotor diameter 14.02m (46ft); length with rotors turning 17.07m (56ft)
Max take-off weight: 5,397kg (11,900lb)
Max speed: 259km/h (161mph)
Max rate of climb: 411m (1,350ft) per minute
Service ceiling: 5,030m (16,500ft)
Operational range: 695km (432 miles) with max payload and standard fuel
Payload: 2,451kg (5,405lb)
History: announced in September 1978 as a twin-turbine variant of the Model 212 with a four-blade main rotor of advanced design, it is Bell's first production helicopter with a four-blade rotor. It entered service in January 1981 with ERA Helicopters of Alaska and provided not only higher performance but less noise and vibration than the 212. The 412SP is the latest commercial variant, and Bell transferred production of the model to Canada in February 1989.

The Bell Model 412SP is used as a flying ambulance, and also by New York City Police Dept

Bell/Boeing V22 Osprey

Country of origin: USA
First flight: 19 March 1989
Type: vertical take-off assault transport
Crew/accommodation: three, and up to 24 troops
Powerplant: two 4,590kW (6,150shp) Allison T406-AD-400 turboshafts
Dimensions: rotor diameter 11.58m (38ft); length with rotors turning 17.65m (57ft 11in)
Max take-off weight: 21,546kg (47,500lb) with vertical take-off
Max speed: 571km/h (359mph) at sea level
Operational radius: 278km (173 miles) with 4,545kg (10,000lb) payload
Payload: up to 6,804kg (15,000lb)
History: the world's first tilt-rotor convertiplane to enter service, derived from Bell's long experience with experimental engines. The engines are at the tips of the wings in vertically-rotating nacelles, in order that the two large-diameter propellers/rotors provide direct lift prior to rotating forward to provide wingborne forward flight. First deliveries, to the US Marines, are planned for 1997.

The V-22 Osprey offers great potential. It was developed under a US Navy contract with Textron Inc's Bell Helicopter unit at Fort Worth, Texas, and by Boeing's Philadelphia

56 *helicopter division*

Boeing Vertol CH-46D Sea Knight

Country of origin: USA
First flight: April 1958
Type: assault transport
Crew/accommodation: three, and 25 troops
Powerplant: two 1,044kW (1,400shp) General Electric T58-GE-10 turboshafts
Dimensions: rotor diameter (both) 15.54m (51ft); length with rotors turning 25.7m (84ft 4in)
Max take-off weight: 10,433kg (23,000lb)
Cruising speed: 266km/h (165mph) at sea level
Operational range: 383km (238 miles) with 2,064kg (4,550lb) payload
Payload: 4,536kg (10,000lb) slung load
History: operated by the US Marines, the Sea Knight has a rear ramp and side doors. It was a development of the commercial Model 107-II, and the first military version entered service in 1965 as the CH-46A, with two 932kW (1,250shp) T58-GE-8D turboshafts, capable of carrying 25 troops. Other variants include the US Navy UH-46 replenishment CH-UH-46D with cambered rotor blades, the CH-46E with 1,394kW (1,890shp) T58-GE-16s, and now the updated CH-46F.

An extensive program of upgrading kits is providing extended life to all versions of the CH-46

Boeing Model 234LR Chinook

Country of origin: USA
First flight: September 1961, as the Model 114
Type: medium/heavy utility and transport
Crew/accommodation: two, and up to 44 passengers
Powerplant: two 3,039kW (4,075shp) Avro Lycoming AL 5512 turboshafts
Dimensions: rotor diameter 18.29m (60ft); length with rotors turning 30.18m (99ft)
Max take-off weight: 22,000kg (48,500lb) loaded
Cruising speed: 269km/h (167mph)
Operational range: 982km (610 miles)
Payload: up to 12,701kg (28,000lb)
History: the Model 234 is the largest-capacity commercial helicopter in service in the Western world, the civil equivalent of the successful military Boeing Model 114 (CH-47 Chinook). First announced in 1978, it used wide-chord fiberglass rotor blades, revised fuselage side fairings, quadricycle landing gear and weather radar housed in a longer nose. The long-range (LR) variant has entered service, but the utility (UT) variant, with two internal fuel tanks and a 24-passenger capability, is still to appear.

Boeing 234s are operated by Columbia Helicopters, Oregon, and Norway's Helikopter Service operates two, primarily for transporting oil workers to platforms

Boeing Vertol CH-47D Chinook

Country of origin: USA
First flight: September 1961
Type: medium tactical heavy-lift transport
Crew/accommodation: two, and either 44 troops or 24 litters plus two attendants
Powerplant: two 2,796kW (3,750shp) Textron Lycoming T55-L-712 SSB turboshafts
Dimensions: rotor diameter (both) 18.29m (60ft); fuselage length 15.87m (52ft 1in)
Max take-off weight: 24,494kg (54,000lb)
Max speed: 286km/h (178mph) at sea level
Max rate of climb: 464m (1,522ft) per minute
Service ceiling: 2,575m (8,450ft)
Operational range: 426km (265 miles) at sea level
Payload: external loads of up to 13,916kg (30,679lb)
History: an enlarged and more powerful version of the Model 107, this is the Western world's most important medium/heavy-lift tactical helicopter, with about 650 in military and civil use. It has a rear ramp/door, giving access to the long rectangular-section fuselage.

CH-47 Chinooks are remanufactured and fully modernized by Boeing, Philadelphia. They have more powerful engines and transmissions, all-fiberglass rotor blades, a modularized hydraulic system, and an automatic flight control system

Boeing Sikorsky RAH-66 Comanche

Country of origin: USA
First flight: scheduled for August 1995
Type: armed reconnaissance/light attack/and air combat
Crew/accommodation: two seats in tandem
Powerplant: two 690kW (925shp) LHTEC (Allison & Garrett) T800 turboshafts
Dimensions: rotor diameter 11.9m (39ft 0.5in); fuselage length 13.22m (43ft 4.5in)
Max weight: 4,587kg (10,112lb)
Max speed: 328km/h (203mph)
Combat radius: 2,335km (1,450 miles)
Armament: four AGM-114 Hellfire and two AIM-92 Stinger internal missiles
Payload: 1,185kg (2,612lb)
Avionics: Longbow fire-control radar, passive long-range high-resolution sensors, triple redundant fly-by-wire flight-control system
History: a US Army requirement to use fewer personnel and long range, self-deployable aircraft based in the continental USA has resulted in the RAH-66 armed reconnaissance prototype, commissioned in April 1991. A design review was held in January 1992 and the helicopter is scheduled to enter service in the year 2003.

Features include FANTAIL anti-torque system, a five-blade bearingless main rotor, and self-healing digital mission electronics

Bristol Sycamore HC.Mk 14

Country of origin: UK
First flight: July 1947 as the Type 171 Mk 1
Type: utility and search and rescue
Crew/accommodation: five seats
Powerplant: one 410kW (550shp) Alvis Leonides 73
Dimensions: rotor diameter 14.81m (48ft 7in); fuselage length 14.07m (46ft 2in)
Max take-off weight: 2,540kg (5,600lb)
Max speed: 204km/h (127mph) at sea level
Operational range: 431km (268 miles)
History: the first British-designed helicopter to enter RAF service, the Sycamore was developed from the Type 171 Mk 1 and entered service as the HR.Mk 12 anti-submarine reconnaissance and search and rescue helicopter in February 1952. The HR.Mk 13s were supplied to Fighter Command before the HR.Mk 14s were developed, with additional cabin doors, taller landing gear and other improvements including the relocation of the pilot to the right. The Sycamore was an important step in the early development of helicopter use against guerrilla warfare and was used extensively in Cyprus and Malaya.

The HR.Mk 13s, of which there were two, were equipped with winches for search and rescue service

California Helicopters S 58T

Country of origin: USA
First flight: 1954
Type: passenger lift/heavy lift (external) cargo
Crew/accommodation: two, and up to 14 passengers
Powerplant: twin-turbine Pratt & Whitney Canada PT6T 6
Dimensions: rotor diameter 17.0/m (56ft), length with rotors turning 17.28m (56ft 8.25in); height 4.85m (15ft 11in)
Max take-off weight: 5,896kg (13,000lb)
Max speed: 222km/h (138mph) at sea level
Cruising speed: 204km/h (127mph)
Hovering ceiling: 1,433m (4,700ft)
Operational range: 281km (299 miles)
History: California Helicopters acquired all rights to the S 58T from Sikorsky in December 1981, converting the piston-engined Sikorsky S-58s. These converted helicopters are operated throughout the world in a variety of roles, and both the FAA and British Civil Aviation Authority have approved the aircraft for IFR operation. Now in use with several Air Forces, they are also used for VIP services and New York Airways had four, which were used for shuttle services from Manhattan to the New York airports.

Sikorsky carried out conversions to 146 aircraft prior to selling all manufacturing and spare parts rights to California Helicopters

Cierva Autogyro/Avro Rota Mk 1

Country of origin: Spain/UK
First flight: 1925
Type: utility autogyro
Crew/accommodation: single seat
Powerplant: one 104kW (140hp) Armstrong Siddeley Genet Major 1A air-cooled radial
Dimensions: rotor diameter 11.20m (37ft); fuselage length 6.01m (19ft 8.5in)
Max take-off weight: 816kg (1,800lb)
Max speed: 177km/h (110mph) at sea level
Hovering ceiling: 2,438m (8,000ft)
Operational range: 465km (285 miles)
Payload: up to 169kg (372lb)
History: invented by Juan de la Cierva and brought to England for trials, the C.6A Autogyro was developed under license by Avro. Extensive trials lasted many years before the Type C.90A went into production for the RAF, entering service in 1934 and designated Rota Mk 1. They operated throughout the Second World War in the hands of the School of Army Co-operation until 1945.

The first successful model was the C.4, that first flew in January 1923; successive improvements and developments went on up to C.40, mainly undertaken by Avro in the UK, Liore-et-Olivier in France and Pitcairn in the USA

E H Industries EH 101

Country of origin: UK/Italy
First flight: October 1987
Type: multi-role
Crew/accommodation: one or two crew, plus up to 30 passengers in commercial variant
Powerplant: three 1,278kW (1,714shp) General Electric T700-GE-401A turboshafts
Dimensions: rotor diameter 18.59m (61ft); length with rotors turning 22.81m (74ft 10in)
Max take-off weight: 13,000kg (28,660lb)
Max speed: 309km/h (192mph)
Operational range: estimated with 30 passengers 1,019km (633 miles)
Armament: naval version can carry up to four torpedoes or other weapons; ASV is designed to carry air-to-surface missiles and other weapons
Payload: palletized internal loads or slung loads up to 5,443kg (12,000lb)
History: E H Industries, a partnership between Westland and Agusta, formed in 1980 to develop a new anti-submarine warfare helicopter. Designed to be either land or ship-based, the UK variant uses the Merlin version with Rolls-Royce/Turboméca RTM.322 turboshafts. The naval version is designed to have advanced electronics and weapons. Further developments are planned.

The EH 101 Merlin, about to land on the Type 23 frigate HMS Iron Duke, *during ship interface trials*

Enstrom Model 280 FXA Shark

Country of origin: USA
First flight: December 1983
Type: light helicopter
Crew/accommodation: one, and two passengers side by side on a bench seat
Powerplant: one 168kW (225hp) Textron Lycoming H10-360-FIAD flat four engine with Rotomaster 3BT5EE1032 turbocharger
Dimensions: rotor diameter 9.75m (32ft); fuselage length 8.94m (29ft 4in); height 2.79m (9ft 2in)
Max take-off weight: 1,179kg (2,600lb)
Max speed: 188km/h (117mph)
Cruising speed: 172km/h (107mph)
Max rate of climb: 442m (1,450ft) per minute
Hovering ceiling: 2,345m (7,700ft) at max weight
Operational range: 483km (300 miles)
History: the 280 FXA Shark features completely faired landing gear, and a redesigned air inlet system. The tail has been redesigned to incorporate endplate fins on the horizontal stabilizer, covered tail rotor shaft and a tail rotor guard. New seats include lumbar support and energy-absorbing foam.

Illustrated is the 280 FX Shark, the personal helicopter with a reputed direct running cost of well under US$100 per hour and a purchase price of less than $250,000

Enstrom Model F-28F Falcon

Country of origin: USA
First flight: certification from FAA given January 1981
Type: light helicopter
Crew/accommodation: one, and two passengers
Powerplant: one 168kW (225shp) Lycoming H10-360-FIAD four-cylinder air-cooled turbocharged engine
Dimensions: rotor diameter 9.8m (32ft); fuselage length 8.6m (28ft 1.2in); height 2.7m (9ft)
Max take-off weight: 1,179kg (2,600lb)
Max speed: 180km/h (112mph)
Operational range: 423km (263 miles)
Payload: 467kg (1,030lb)
History: the original basic F-28A was replaced by the turbocharged version F-28C in 1975. Production of the F-28C ceased in 1981, and it was replaced by the F-28F as described above. An Enstrom wet or dry dispersal agricultural kit is available as two side-mounted hoppers, with large quick-fill openings and spray beams. The F-28F is fitted with a 159-litre (35Imp gal/42US gal) fuel tank.

Illustrated is the F-28F-P Sentinel, a dedicated police patrol version of the F-28F developed for the Pasadena Police Department in California, which took delivery of its first F-28F-P in 1986

Eurocopter NH90

Country of origin: France, Germany, Italy and the Netherlands
First flight: scheduled for Fall 1995
Type: tactical transport
Crew/accommodation: two, and up to 20 troops
Powerplant: RTM 322, GE CT7 6 turboshafts
Dimensions: rotor diameter 16.3m (53ft 4in); length with rotors turning 19.6m (64ft 3.7in)
Max take-off weight: 9,100kg (20,065.5lb)
Cruising speed: 260km/h (161.46mph)
Operational range: 4 hours' endurance
Payload: 2,000kg (4,410lb)
Avionics: fly by wire controls; digital Mil-Bus concepts, allowing a modular integrated and flexible system
History: development work began within weeks of approval by the steering committee in March 1992, with the maiden flight scheduled for 1995 and the first production unit due by end 1999. Two main versions are planned for this medium-size helicopter. The tactical transport variant for 14 combat-ready troops will also have SAR and casualty evacuation capabilities in peacetime, while the NATO frigate helicopter will include ASW and anti-surface unit warfare equipped with torpedoes, and have SAR and material transport capabilities.

The NH90 will offer high reliability and low maintenance costs

Eurocopter Tiger

Country of origin: France and Germany
First flight: deliveries due to begin in 1997
Type: anti-tank
Crew/accommodation: two
Powerplant: two 1,160kW (1,556shp) Turboméca/MTU/Rolls-Royce 2MTR 390 turboshafts
Dimensions: rotor diameter 13.41m (44ft); length with rotors turning 16.18m (53ft 1in)
Max take-off weight: 5,600kg (12,348lb)
Max speed: 300km/h (188mph) or 272km/h (169mph) in armed configuration
Cruising speed: 232km/h (144mph)
Max rate of climb: 10.7m (35.1ft) per second
Operational range: 800km (496.8 miles)
Armament: four Mistral or Stinger fire and forget anti-tank missiles, plus eight MOT
Avionics: automatic flight control system
History: funded by France and Germany in order to fulfill the requirements of their respective armies, the Tiger anti-tank and Gerfaut combat support variants are both capable of combat in a wide variety of environments and temperature conditions in Europe and overseas; they retain their full combat capability in NBC conditions and continue safe flight after nuclear electromagnetic pulse.

The Tiger is capable of defeating all current and projected armored
80 *vehicles*

Eurocopter AS 565 AA Panther

Country of origin: France/Germany
First flight: February 1984 as prototype SA 365M Panther
Type: light tactical transport
Crew/accommodation: two, and ten commandoes
Powerplant: two 660kW (783shp) Turboméca Arriel 1 M1 Super Contingency power (O.E.I.) turboshafts
Dimensions: rotor diameter 11.94m (39ft 2in); length with rotors turning 13.68m (44ft 11in)
Max take-off weight: 4,250kg (9,369lb)
Max speed: 287km/h (178.23mph)
Max rate of climb: 5.8m/second (1,141ft/minute)
Operational range: 860km (523 miles)
Payload: 1,600kg (3,527lb) with sling
History: the AS 565 UA was developed as the utility version of the Panther for light tactical transport and casualty-carrying missions. The AS 565 AA is an armed version, equipped with 20mm (0.78in) pod-mounted cannons, rocket-launchers and machine-guns; the navy version for search and rescue is designated AS 565 MA. Finally, there is an armed navalized version for anti-surface vessel attack or for anti-submarine warfare, designated AS 565 SA.

The Panther is a twin-engined multi-role helicopter, in the 4-tonne (8,829lb) class

Eurocopter AS 550 U2 Fennec

Country of origin: France/Germany
First flight: June 1974 as prototype Ecureuil
Type: reconnaissance observation
Crew/accommodation: one, and five troops
Powerplant: one 546kW (732shp) Turboméca Arriel 1 D1
Dimensions: main rotor diameter 10.69m (35ft 1in); length with rotors turning 12.94m (42ft 5.5in)
Max take-off weight: 2,500kg (5,512lb) with external load
Max speed: 287km/h (178mph)
Max rate of climb: 8.8m/second (1,730ft/minute)
Operational range: 656km (407 miles)
Payload: 1,160kg (2,557lb) slung load
History: the utility version of the single engined Fennec is used for reconnaissance and observation, being ideally suited for hot-and-high operations. The AS 550 C2 Butterfield version can be equipped with axial weapons, including cannon, rocket-launchers and machine-guns or side-firing cannon. The AS 550 C2 is the anti-tank variant. A twin-engined AS 555 UN/AN/MN/SN variant is also produced.

AS 555 UN Fennec, powered by two Turboméca TM319 Arrius turbine engines, with full authority digital engine control (FADEC)

Kaman SH-2F Sea Sprite

Country of origin: USA
First flight: 1962
Type: naval shipborne anti-submarine
Crew/accommodation: three crew
Powerplant: two 1,812kW (1,350shp) General Electric T58-GE-8F turboshafts
Dimensions: rotor diameter 13.4m (44ft); length with rotors turning 16m (52ft 6in)
Max take-off weight: 6,124kg (13,500lb)
Max speed: 266km/h (165mph) at sea level
Operational range: 679km (422 miles)
Armament: two lightweight anti-submarine torpedoes carried out to 65km (40 miles) from ship, with up to 72 minutes' loiter on station
Payload: 2,955kg (6,500lb)
History: originating as the HU-2K which first entered service in 1962 with the US Navy as a utility helicopter, it was built in considerable numbers, and the SH-2D became the primary anti-submarine and unarmed rescue helicopter for smaller warships. Early variants were powered by a single T58 turboshaft. The Department of Defense scrapped the UH-2 (it had been redesignated) program in the 1960s, but after production was reopened the first SH-2F was delivered to the Navy on 7 December 1983.

The SH-2F should remain in fleet service into the next century

Kamov Ka-25 'Hormone-A'

Country of origin: USSR
First flight: entered service in 1965
Type: anti-submarine
Crew/accommodation: five seats
Powerplant: two 671kW (900shp) Glushenkov GTD-3BM
Dimensions: rotor diameter (both) 15.74m (51ft 8in); fuselage length 9.75m (32ft 10in)
Max take-off weight: 7,500kg (16,534lb)
Cruising speed: 193km/h (120mph) at sea level
Operational range: 400km (249 miles)
Armament: two 406mm (15.98in) or 450mm (17.72in) torpedoes or depth charges (either conventional or nuclear) carried internally, or one wire-guided torpedo carried in a semi-external housing.
History: these compact helicopters are ideal for small ship platforms and were derived from the Ka-20 prototypes of 1960. Production ceased in 1975 after some 450 Ka-25s had been built over the three versions. The Hormone A has a 'Big-Bulge' search radar, 'Tie-Rod' optronic sensor and sonobuoys with either dunking sonar or towed MAD.

Following its first flight, the Ka-25 was quickly developed into its three variants; the twin rotors are clearly shown in this picture

Kamov Ka-25 'Hormone-C'

Country of origin: USSR
First flight: about 1960
Type: search and rescue
Crew/accommodation: three crew
Powerplant: two 738kW (990shp) Glushenkov GTD-3BM
Dimensions: rotor diameter (both) 15.74m (51ft 7.7in); fuselage length 9.75m (32ft)
Max take-off weight: 7,500kg (16,353lb)
Max speed: 220km/h (137mph) at sea level
Operational range: 650km (404 miles)
Payload: 12 survivors or unknown number of litters plus attendant, or freight
History: the Hormone-C has a pair of superimposed contra-rotating rotors and was designed as a compact shipboard helicopter and established a good reputation for reliability and overall weight-lifting capability. Hormone-A is the designated anti-submarine variant, Hormone-B the missile-targeting. The Hormone-C also operates in a utility and plane guard capacity, in addition to SAR and is equipped with search radar housed in an undernose radome, a searchlight, and loudspeaker.

A typical Kamov helicopter configuration, compact and yet capacious, with twin contra-rotating rotors

Kamov Ka-26 'Hoodlum'

Country of origin: USSR
First flight: 1965
Type: light general purpose
Crew/accommodation: two, and six passengers
Powerplant: two 242.5kW (325shp) Vedeneyev M-14V-26
Dimensions: rotor diameter (both) 13m (42ft 8in); fuselage length 7.75m (25ft 5in)
Max take-off weight: 3,250kg (7,165lb)
Cruising speed: 150km/h (93mph) at sea level
Operational range: 399km (248 miles)
Payload: up to 1,065kg (2,348lb) freight internally, or 1,100kg (2,425lb) slung load
History: the 'Hoodlum' civil helicopter conforms to the well-proven Kamov practice of two co-axial contra-rotating tri-bladed rotors shed above a box-shaped airplane-type fuselage with large tail surfaces. It is used primarily used for agricultural roles, and can be fitted with dusters, spray bars or a chemical hopper; the Ka-26 can also be used as a flying crane and in firefighting, resources exploration support and cable-laying.

Cockpit shot of the Ka-26, a civil helicopter with virtually no paramilitary applications

Kamov Ka-27 'Helix-A'

Country of origin: USSR
First flight: about 1979
Type: anti-submarine
Crew/accommodation: five seats
Powerplant: two 1,659kW (2,225shp) Isotov TV3-11/V turboshafts
Dimensions: rotor diameter (both) 15.9m (52ft 2in); fuselage length 11.3m (37ft 1in)
Max take-off weight: 12,600kg (27,778lb)
Cruising speed: 230km/h (143mph) at sea level
Operational range: 800km (497 miles)
Armament: two torpedoes or depth charges, either conventional or nuclear, carried internally
Payload: up to 5,000kg (11,023lb) slung load
History: introduced as a successor to the Ka-25, the Ka-27 is of the same basic design though larger and more powerful, yet still able to fit into the hangar space designed for the Ka-25. The Helix-A is capable of carrying an infantry squad or freight in addition to its torpedo armament. Sensors include surveillance radar, dunking sonar, towed MAD and directional ESM.

Designed as a compact shipboard successor to the Ka-25, the Helix-A is the highly-reliable anti-submarine version

Kamov Ka-27 'Helix-B'

Country of origin: USSR
First flight: entered service 1982
Type: light assault transport
Crew/accommodation: three, and 16 troops
Powerplant: two 1,660kW (2,226shp) Isotov TV3-117V
Dimensions: rotor diameter (both) 15.9m (52ft 2in); fuselage length 11.3m (37ft 0.9in)
Max take-off weight: 12,600kg (27,778lb)
Cruising speed: 222km/h (138mph)
Operational range: 800km (497 miles)
Payload: up to 4,000kg (8,818lb) of internally-carried freight or 5,000kg (11,023lb) of externally-carried weight
History: all Ka-27 'Helix' models feature the normal Kamov arrangement of superimposed coaxial tri-blade rotors turning in opposite directions – this removes any torque problem that would occur with the short un-rotored tail. One advantage of this feature is the smaller hangar space these models require on board ships, where space is limited. The Helix B is a development of the Ka-27 not possible with the smaller Ka-25.

The Ka-27 has since been developed into the Ka-32 civil version, and is
seen here in Aeroflot markings

Kamov Ka-50 'Werewolf'

Country of origin: USSR
First flight: 17 June 1982
Type: daylight anti-tank
Crew/accommodation: two crew
Powerplant: two 1,640kW (2,200shp) Klimov TV3-117VK turboshafts
Dimensions: rotor diameter (both) 14.5m (47ft 6in); length with rotors turning 16.35m (53ft 7in)
Max take-off weight: 5,450kg (12,000lb)
Max speed: 349km/h (217mph)
Combat radius: 232km (144 miles)
Armament: 16 Vikhr (AT-9 Whirlwind) anti-tank laser-beam riding missiles in two clusters of eight; AS-12 Kegler series missiles, FAB500 bombs and twin 23mm (1in) cannon pods, up to 80 S8 80mm (3.15in) air to ground rockets, and a UV-26 chaff and flare dispenser
Avionics: include four EA Orbita computers, handling a display system, navigation control, mission control, link up and back up
History: renamed 'Werewolf' by Kamov, the Ka-50 was designed to outperform the McDonnell Douglas AH-64 Apache and is the Soviets' latest combat helicopter. It has been known in the West since 1984. At the MosAeroshow in 1992, the Ka-50 made its first public appearance, but under its project code of V-80.

The Ka-50's local name is the Vertolyet-80

McDonnell Douglas AH-64A Apache

Country of origin: USA
First flight: September 1975, as the Model 77
Type: advanced attack helicopter
Crew/accommodation: two crew
Powerplant: two 1,265kW (1,696shp) General Electric T700-GE-701 turboshafts
Dimensions: rotor diameter 14.63m (48ft); length with rotors turning 17.76m (58ft 3.2in)
Max take-off weight: 9,525kg (21,000lb)
Max speed: 365km/h (227mph)
Max rate of climb: 762m (2,500ft) per minute
Hovering ceiling: 4,570m (15,000ft)
Operational range: 482km (300 miles)
Armament: McDonnell Douglas M230 Chain Gun 30mm (1.2in) automatic cannon; four underwing hardpoints with Aircraft Hydro-Forming pylons and ejector units carrying up to 16 Rockwell Hellfire anti-tank missiles or up to 76 70mm (2.76in) folding-fin rockets in their launchers
History: selection of the AH-64 for the US Army was announced in December 1976, and named Apache in 1981. The first aircraft were delivered in 1984, air-to-air Sidewinder missiles were successfully fired in 1989, and Stinger missile control integration began in 1990.

The first AH-64D Longbow Apache prototype being flight tested in Mesa, Arizona

100

McDonnell Douglas MD-500L

Country of origin: USA
First flight: 28 January 1982
Type: civil light helicopter
Crew/accommodation: one, and six passengers
Powerplant: one 313kW (420shp) Allison 250 C20B turboshaft
Dimensions: rotor diameter 8.03m (26ft 4in); length with rotors turning 9.4m (30ft 10in)
Max take-off weight: 1,610kg (3,550lb)
Max speed: 282km/h (175mph) at sea level
Cruising speed: 258km/h (160mph) at sea level
Max rate of climb: 572m (1,875ft) per minute
Hovering ceiling: 2,590m (8,500ft)
Operational range: 473km (294 miles)
History: replaced the MD-500D in 1982 as the basic US production version, being a longer and more streamlined development. Other civil versions include the 520N with NOTAR ® tailboom, and 530F lifter intended for operation at high altitudes or high temperatures, and the 530N-modified MD530 with NOTAR ® tailboom. The MD-530F has the 485kW (650shp) Allison 250-C30 turboshaft, rotors are 0.15m (6in) longer, and the overall length is increased by 0.38m (1ft 3in); this first flew in October 1982.

Washington DC police use the MD-500Es to patrol the nation's capital

McDonnell Douglas MD-520 Notar™

Country of origin: USA
First flight: 7 December 1981
Type: utility
Crew/accommodation: five seats
Powerplant: one 336kW (450shp) Allison 250-C20R turboshaft
Dimensions: rotor diameter 8.3m (27ft 4.8in); fuselage length with rotors turning 9.78m (32ft 1.2in); height 2.7m (8ft 8in)
Max take-off weight: 1,746kg (3,850lb) with external load
Max speed: 282km/h (175mph)
Hovering ceiling: 6,097m (20,000ft)
Operational range: 382km (239 miles) at sea level
Payload: 000kg (1,704lb), with external load, 1,027kg (2,264lb)
History: the NOTAR™ designation stands for NO Tail Rotor, and is a significant breakthrough in helicopter design, dispensing with the small rear rotor and using the blast of the jet engine to maintain stability. It is also claimed that this reduction to the number of moving parts cuts operating costs and noise levels.

The McDonnell Douglas MD-520N helicopter with the Notar® no-tail rotor system for anti-torque and
directional control clearly shown

McDonnell Douglas MD-530 MG Defender

Country of origin: USA
First flight: May 1984
Type: light attack
Crew/accommodation: two crew
Powerplant: one 317kW (425shp) Allison 250 series turboshaft
Dimensions: rotor diameter 8.05m (26ft 5in); fuselage length 7.29m (23ft 11in)
Max take-off weight: 1,406kg (3,100lb)
Max speed: 241km/h (150mph)
Operational range: 333km (207 miles) at sea level
Armament: provision for four Stringer AAMs, four TOW anti-armor missiles, four 12-tube rocket launchers and/or one 7.62mm (0.3in) MD Chain Gun or 12.7mm (0.5cal/0.4953in) machine gun
History: originally the Hughes 500M Defender; McDonnell Douglas acquired Hughes in January 1984, and continued development. US Army designations are AH-6 and MH-6. Variants are the 500MG Defender, as 530MG above but with 313kW (420shp) Allison 250-C20B turboshaft, and the MD-500E. The paramilitary MG Defender was introduced in July 1985, and the Nightfox in January 1986 for night surveillance.

An MD-530N helicopter in military camouflage undergoes flight tests near Mesa, Arizona

McDonnell Douglas MDX

Country of origin: USA/Australia
First flight: 18 December 1992
Type: utility commercial
Crew/accommodation: eight or ten seats
Powerplant: two 450kW (603shp) Pratt & Whitney Canada PW206A turboshafts
Dimensions: rotor diameter 8.33m (27ft 4.8in); fuselage length 7.62m (25ft)
Max take-off weight: 3,065kg (6,690lb)
Max speed: 322km/h (200mph) at sea level
Max rate of climb: 14.2m/sec (2,800ft/minute)
Operational range: 599km (372 miles)
Payload: 1,163kg (2,565lb)
History: certification is scheduled for October 1994, for the first new helicopter to be committed to production for nearly a decade. Orders already stand at 250 units. It features McDonnell Douglas' NOTAR™ system of anti-torque and directional control, successfully introduced on the 520N helicopter since 1991. The outer surface of the fuselage is made of all composite materials, enabling increased payload for size. The MDX also features 1.25m (50in) sliding side-loading doors and a collective-mounted manual override for the automatic fuel control.

An artist's rendering of the MD Explorer, the first commercial helicopter to be committed to production in the 1990s

108

McDonnell Douglas OH-6A Cayuse

Country of origin: USA
First flight: 1960
Type: civil and military light utility
Crew/accommodation: one, and four passengers
Powerplant: one 187kW (250shp) Allison 250-C18 turboshaft
Dimensions: rotor diameter 8.03m (26ft 4in); length with rotors turning 9.24m (30ft 3.5in)
Max take-off weight: 1,080kg (2,400lb)
Cruising speed: 200km/h (125mph) at 1,524m (5,000ft)
Operational range: 611km (380 miles), full load
Payload: up to 353kg (780lb)
History: Hughes developed the Model 369 as a prototype for the US Army in the early 1960s and despite competition from the Bell Model 205 and the Hiller Model 1100, it won, and very large production orders were placed for the OH-6A Cayuse service version. Hughes ran into problems with delivery rates and rising costs, and the program ended when around 1,400 had been delivered. The type was also produced in a civil version, Model 500, later upgraded to the 530, after McDonnell Douglas bought Hughes.

The Hughes Model 500 civil variant seated two including the pilot forward, with two or three behind

MBB BO 105

Country of origin: Germany
First flight: February 1967
Type: all-weather attack light helicopter
Crew/accommodation: one, and four troops
Powerplant: two 313kW (400shp) Allison 250-C20B turboshafts
Dimensions: rotor diameter 9.84m (32ft 3.5in), overall length 11.86m (38ft 11in)
Max take-off weight: 2,500kg (5,512lb)
Max speed: 268km/h (167mph)
Operational range: 555km (345 miles)
Armament: provision for up to six Euromissile HOT missiles or eight TOW anti-armor missiles with stabilizer sight, with gun pod in turret
Payload: 900kg (1,984lb) slung load
History: the basic design has been used for over 30 years, with the CB4 model described above complemented by the CBS4 multi-purpose helicopter, which is capable of carrying an extra passenger in high-density configuration for applications such as executive transport, offshore, and law enforcement/police. The LSA3, fitted with two 373kW (500shp) Allison 250-C28B engines, has a maximum take-off weight of 2,600kg (5,732lb), but the range is reduced to 515km (320 miles).

The BO 105CBS twin-engined light helicopter, equipped for emergency medical services with two litters and seats for pilot and medical crew

MBB BK 117

Country of origin: Germany/Japan
First flight: June 1979
Type: light multi-purpose
Crew/accommodation: one, and seven passengers, or ten in high-density configuration
Powerplant: two 410kW (550shp) Avco Lycoming LTS 101-750B-1
Dimensions: rotor diameter 11m (36ft 1in); length with rotors turning 12.98m (42ft 7in)
Max take-off weight: 3,200kg (7,055lb)
Max speed: 248km/h (154mph) at max weight
Operational range: 550km (342 miles)
Payload: 1,200kg (2,646lb) slung load
History: MBB and Kawasaki agreed to collaborate on the BK 117 in 1977, using the rotor head of the BO 105 and the transmission of the Kawasaki KH-7. The BK 117D1 described above is conventional in basic layout, but unusual in that it has a wide cabin/cargo compartment with a secondary cargo compartment at the rear of the pod section. The helicopter sales of MBB have been combined with Aérospatiale's under the Eurocopter banner, and it is hoped that increased sales will be found for this versatile helicopter.

A BK 117C1 multi-purpose light helicopter, equipped with Turboméca Arriel 1E engines, as opposed to the normal Lycoming LTS 101-750B-1 engines for the base model

Mil Mi-4 'Hound-A'

Country of origin: USSR
First flight: May 1952
Type: military troop/utility transport
Crew/accommodation: three, and up to 14 troops
Powerplant: one 1,700hp Shvetson ASh-82V air-cooled radial
Dimensions: rotor diameter 21m (68ft 11in)
Max take-off weight: 7,800kg (17,200lb)
Cruising speed: 160km/h (99mph) at sea level
Operational ceiling: 4,200m (13,780ft)
Operational range: 595km (370 miles) with full payload
Payload: up to 1,600kg (3,525lb)
History: an early conventional piston-engined helicopter, developed by the Soviet Union and produced throughout the 1950s and 1960s to an estimated total of 3,500 craft. Mainly employed in an unarmed military transport role, the type also served extensively in civil form and was produced under license in the Republic of China, designated Zhi-5. The Mi-4 gave way to the upgraded turbo-powered variant, the Mi-8 'Hip'.

The Mil Mi-4 Hound was a large and industrious workhorse of the Soviet Union, in both military and civil roles

Mil Mi-6 'Hook'

Country of origin: USSR
First flight: 1957
Type: heavy transport
Crew/accommodation: five, and 65-90 passengers or 70 combat-equipped troops
Powerplant: two 4,101kW (5,500shp) Soloviev D-25V (TV- 2BM) turboshafts
Dimensions: rotor diameter 35m (114ft 10in); length with rotors turning 41.74m (136ft 11.5in); height 9.86m (32ft 4in)
Max take-off weight: 38,400kg (84,657lb)
Max speed: 300km/h (186mph)
Hovering ceiling: 4,500m (14,750ft)
Operational range: 1,450km (900 miles)
Armament: some military Mi-6s are fitted with a 12.7mm (0.5in) machine gun in the fuselage nose
Payload: 12,000kg (26,450lb) internally and 8,000kg (17,637lb) slung load
Avionics: all-weather instrumentation, VHF and HF communications radio, three-channel autopilot
History: the world's largest helicopter when first announced in 1957, the Mi-6 later developed into the Mi-10 and Mi-10K flying crane, then the Mi-12 of 1967. Over 800 were built, and standard equipment includes an electric winch of 800kg (1,765lb) capacity, and a central hatch in the cabin floor for a cargo sling.

A prime example of the Soviets' thinking big

Mil Mi-8 'Hip'

Country of origin: USSR
First flight: 1961
Type: medium general-purpose
Crew/accommodation: two, and 24 troops or 28 passengers
Powerplant: two 1,267kW (1,700shp) Isotov TV2-117A turboshafts
Dimensions: rotor diameter 21.29m (69ft 10.2in); length with rotors turning 25.24m (82ft 9.75in)
Max take-off weight: 12,000kg (26,455lb)
Cruising speed: 225km/h (140mph)
Operational range: 500km (311 miles)
Payload: 4,000kg (8,818lb) freight carried internally or 3,000kg (6,614lb) slung load
History: basically a turbine-powered version of the Mi-4, and originally flown with a single 2,013kW (2,700shp) Soloviev turboshaft driving a four-blade main rotor. It was then reissued with the Isotov turboshafts driving a five-blade rotor and first flew in September 1962 in this configuration; variants are the Mi-8T utility, with up to 24 seats and provision for internal and external freight and the Mi-8 Salon with VIP accommodation for 11 passengers and the military versions 'Hip-C' assault transport, 'Hip-E' armed support, 'Hip-F' anti-tank, and 'Hip-D, G, J and K' electronic warfare.

Military Mi-8; circular cabin windows and weapons on outriggers

Mil Mi-17 'Hip-H'

Country of origin: USSR
First flight: 1961 as 'Hip-A'
Type: assault transport
Crew/accommodation: two/three, and up to 24 troops or 28 passengers
Powerplant: two 1,420kW (1,900shp) Isotov TV3-117MT turboshafts
Dimensions: rotor diameter 21.29m (69ft 10in); fuselage length 18.31m (60ft 1in); height 5.65m (18ft 6.5in)
Max take-off weight: 12,260kg (27,000lb)
Max speed: 270km/h (168mph)
Operational range: 467km (290 miles)
Armament: one 12.7mm (0.5in) machine gun in the nose, plus up to six rocket packs and four AT-2 'Swatter' anti-armor missiles

Developed from the Mi-8 general utility helicopter, the Mi-17 'Hip-H' is a relatively simple upgrade, and is now a very widely-used helicopter with over 10,000 'Hip-C' variants produced. The 'Hip-H' detailed above is still being produced in large quantities, powered by a pair of turboshafts positioned above the cabin and geared together to drive the single five-bladed rotor.

The Mi-17 'Hip-H', a relatively simple upgrade of the Mi-8, with better performance in hot-and-high conditions

Mil Mi-24 'Hind-D'

Country of origin: USSR
First flight: entered service 1974
Type: assault helicopter
Crew/accommodation: two, and eight troops
Powerplant: two 1,640kW (2,200shp) Isotov TV-117 turboshafts
Dimensions: rotor diameter 17m (55ft 9in); length with rotors turning 21m (68ft 11in)
Max take-off weight: 10,940kg (24,100lb)
Cruising speed: 295km/h (183mph) with weapons
Max rate of climb: 900m (2,953ft) per minute
Combat radius: 225km (140 miles)
Armament: one four-barrel 12.7mm (0.5in) gun turret under the nose, four UV-32-57 57mm (2.25in) rocket launcher pods and four AT-2 'Swatter' IR homing anti-armor missiles
Avionics: comprehensive electronic flight-control and engine-management systems with communications and all-weather navaids
History: first identified in 1976 appearing with an entirely redesigned nose and with the pilot and weapons operator being seated in tandem, unlike the previous Hind variants produced since the mid-1960s in very large numbers.

The Hind D, E and F battlefield support helicopters followed the Hind A, B and C assault transport series into service in the mid-1970s

Mil Mi-24 'Hind F'

Country of origin: USSR
First flight: mid-1960s as the 'Hind-A'
Type: dedicated anti-armor attack
Crew/accommodation: two, and provision for an anti-tank team in emergencies
Powerplant: two 1,640kW (2,200shp) Isotov TV3-117 turboshafts
Dimensions: rotor diameter 16.76m (55ft); fuselage length 16.9m (55ft 6in)
Max take-off weight: 11,000kg (24,420lb)
Max speed: 322km/h (200mph)
Operational range: 225km (140 miles)
Armament: twin-barrel GSh-30L 30mm (1.25in) cannon on the starboard side of the nose, four folding-fin AT-6 'Spiral' anti-armor missiles on the stub-wing strongpoints and 57mm (2.25in) rocket launcher pads
Avionics: enlarged radar designator used with the tube launchers for enhanced target acquisition, plus IR jamming and suppression systems
History: the latest derivative of the Hind series of helicopters is the Mi-24 'Hind-F' The Mi-24 can generally be regarded as the world's best combat helicopter. The Mi-25 is the export version of the Mi-24, and over 3,000 have been exported outside of the Warsaw Pact countries.

The series of 'Hind' helicopters developed from the mid-1960s includes the Mi-24, Mi-25 and Mi-35, all with cockpits in tandem

Mil Mi-26 'Halo'

Country of origin: USSR
First flight: December 1977
Type: military heavy lift/assault
Crew/accommodation: five, and 85 troops
Powerplant: two 8,500kW (11,400shp)
Lotarev D-136 free-turbine turboshafts
Dimensions: rotor diameter 32m (104ft
11.8in); length with rotors turning 40.025m
(131ft 3.8in); height 8.15m (26ft 8.7in)
Max take-off weight: 56,000kg (123,457lb)
Max speed: 295km/h (183mph) at sea level
Cruising speed: 255km/h (158mph)
Hovering ceiling: 1,800m (5,906ft)
Operational range: 800km (497 miles)
Payload: up to 20,000kg (44,090lb)
Avionics: advanced multi-channel flight-
control system with powerful autostabilization
and autohover capability at any desired height
History: the Halo is the heaviest and most
powerful helicopter in the world, and was
designed to fulfill the Soviets' need for battlefield heavy-lift and for the opening-up of the
underdeveloped regions, especially the Tyumen
region of Siberia. The Halo has an eight-blade
rotor, with a hub of forged high-strength titanium alloy.

*Similar in size and configuration to
the Mi-6, the Mi-26 Halo has a*
smaller diameter main rotor

Mil Mi-28 'Havoc'

Country of origin: USSR
First flight: 1983
Type: attack helicopter
Crew/accommodation: two crew
Powerplant: two 1,865kW (2,500shp) Isotov TV3-117- related turboshafts
Dimensions: rotor diameter 17m (55ft 9in), fuselage length 17.4m (57ft 1 in)
Max take-off weight: 9,100kg (20,060lb)
Max speed: 299km/h (186mph)
Combat radius: 241km (150 miles)
Armament: one nose barbette-mounted 23mm (1in) cannon, two tube-launched air-to-air missiles and four laser-guided anti-armor missiles
Avionics: IR suppressors and IR decoy devices, including a pulsed jammer
History: the Mi-28 entered service in 1977, with attack helicopter regiments of the Soviet armed forces. Believed to be very comparable to the US Army AH-64 Apache, with full air-to-air and air-to-ground facilities, the Havoc has a slim, deep fuselage with a large bulged nose. Cockpits are in tandem, with the pilot seated behind the gunner.

The Mi-26 is believed to have undergone trials in operational conditions in Afghanistan in 1985, entering full service late in 1987, with attack helicopter regiments of the Soviet Forces

Orlando/Sikorsky S 55 Heli-Camper

Country of origin: USA
First flight: Sikorsky prototype YH-19 1949
Type: VIP model
Crew/accommodation: one, and four passengers
Powerplant: one 596kW (800shp) Wright Cyclone R-1300-3D piston engine
Dimensions: rotor diameter 16.16m (53ft); length with rotors turning 18.91m (62ft 0.5in)
Max take-off weight: 3,266kg (7,200lb)
Cruising speed: 145km/h (90mph)
Operational range: 563km (350 miles)
History: Orlando Helicopter Airways produces several remanufactured models of the Sikorsky S-55/H-19 and S-58/H34 series helicopters. The VIP Model offers a fully-carpeted and soundproofed cabin, hot and cold water, refrigerator, two-burner stove, shower, washbasin and toilet plus air conditioning, color television and AM/FM stereo radio and tape deck, together with many other luxury trimmings in the stripped and remanufactured airframe. Other variants include the Vistaplane 8-11 passenger/air ambulance, taking up to six litters plus two attendants; Nite-Writer aerial advertising model and the Bearcat agricultural wet and dry spray model.

An S-58 built as a replacement for the S-55, and now in five variants

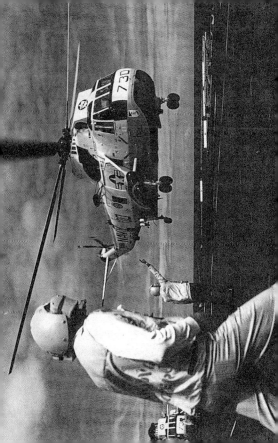

Robinson R22 Beta

Country of origin: USA
First flight: entered production 1979
Type: lightweight civil
Crew/accommodation: one, one passenger alongside
Powerplant: one 119kW (160hp) Textron Lycoming O-320-B2C flat-four engine
Dimensions: rotor diameter 7.67m (25ft 2in); length with rotors turning 8.76m (28ft 9in)
Max take-off weight: 621kg (1,370lb)
Max speed: 190km/h (118mph)
Cruising speed: 177km/h (110mph)
Max rate of climb: 305m (1,000ft) per minute
Hovering ceiling: 2,125m (6,970ft)
Operational range: 592km (368 miles)
Payload: 242kg (535lb)
History: Robinson began development of the R22 in 1973, and six years later received certification. The R22 series has become one of the best-selling civil helicopters with deliveries currently running at about 500 units per year. It offers a high degree of performance and reliability, simple maintenance and low operating costs. The R22 operates in more than 25 countries, and is available as Beta, Mariner (equipped with floats), IFR Trainer (especially-designed for instrument flight training) and Police, available with dual searchlights, PA speaker and siren.

Robinson R44 Astro

Country of origin: USA
First flight: March 1990
Type: light civil utility
Crew/accommodation: one, and three passengers seated as two-plus-two
Powerplant: one 194kW (260hp) Textron Lycoming O 540
Dimensions: rotor diameter 11.9m (33ft); length with rotors turning 11.6m (38ft 2in)
Max take-off weight: 1,088kg (2,400lb)
Cruising speed: 209km/h (130mph)
Max rate of climb: 305m (1,000ft) per minute
Hovering ceiling: 1,858m (6,100ft)
Operational range: 249km (400 miles)
Payload: 640kg (1,000lb)
History: Robinsons' second helicopter is now in production. A four seat version of the successful R22, it is a new design with virtually no commonality of parts, aimed at filling the civil helicopter requirement gap between their R22 and the light turbine machines. Reasonably priced, the R44 should find a ready market and initial orders look encouraging, but customer reaction to operational helicopters will be the proving point.

Larger than the R22, the R44 four-seat helicopter is now with dealers and deliveries to customers start in 1994

Saro (Saunders-Roe) Skeetor T.Mk 12

Country of origin: UK
First flight: 1948 as the W.14 Skeeter 1
Type: training helicopter
Crew/accommodation: two seats
Powerplant: one 140kW (200hp) de Havilland Gipsy Major 200 Mk 30
Dimensions: rotor diameter 9.75m (32ft); fuselage length 8.08m (26ft 6in)
Max take-off weight: 998kg (2,200lb)
Max speed: 162km/h (101mph) at sea level
Operational range: 346km (215 miles)
History: Saro bought out the Cierva company in 1951, and continued development of the W.14 Skeeter 1. The Skeeter 2 had already been produced with a Gipsy Major 10 engine, the Skeeter 3 used a Gipsy Major 8, and the Skeeter 4 a 134kW (180hp) Blackburn Bombardier 702, which had also been used in later models of the Skeeter 3. The Skeeter 5 was the first really successful helicopter in the series powered by a Gipsy Major 200 Mk 3; it overcame the ground resonance problems encountered with the previous prototype Skeeters and paved the way for service evaluation types, designated Skeeter AOP Mk 10 (three aircraft) and Skeeter T.Mk 11 dual control trainer (one aircraft).

A total of 64 production Mk 12s was produced and these were used by the RAF up to 1964

138

Sikorsky Hoverfly Mk II

Country of origin: USA
First flight: early 1940s
Type: utility
Crew/accommodation: one, and one passenger
Powerplant: one 183kW (245hp) Franklin O-405-9
Dimensions: rotor diameter 11.58m (38ft); fuselage length 10.39m (34ft 1in)
Max take-off weight: 1,175kg (2,590lb)
Max speed: 154km/h (96mph) at sea level
Operational range: five hours' endurance
Armament: none
History: the first helicopter in service with the RAF, the Hoverfly Mk I was part of the Sikorsky VS-316A (R 4) production, powered by a 149kW (200hp) Warner R-550 radial, and delivered to the RAF in 1945 for training. These were followed by the more advanced VS-316B (R-6A) or Hoverfly Mk IIs, which were 22.53km/h (14mph) faster and could be fitted with either floats or wheels. In 1946, 26 were delivered to the RAF and Fleet Air Arm, and were employed in an artillery observation role in addition to their training role.

The Sikorsky R-6A, of which 193
were produced in total

Sikorsky S-58/H-34A Choctaw

Country of origin: USA
First flight: March 1954
Type: military assault/transport
Crew/accommodation: two, and up to 18 troops
Powerplant: one 1,136kW (1,525hp) Wright R 1820 84 cyclone air-cooled radial
Dimensions: rotor diameter 17.07m (56ft); length with rotors turning 22.68m (74ft 5in)
Max take-off weight: 6,038kg (13,300lb)
Cruising speed: 158km/h (98mph) at sea level
Operational ceiling: 2,896m (9,500ft)
Operational range: 293km (182 miles)
Payload: 1,878kg (4,140lb)
History: designed to replace the HO4S in naval service, the S-58 first entered service with the US Navy and the Marine Corps on the HSS-1 Seabat and HUS-1 Seahorse and as the H-34 for the US Army and Air Force, all of which were powered by variants of the Wright R-1820. Total production was almost to reach 2,000 aircraft, with steadily-improving features. Some civil variants were produced, and it was built under license in the UK as the Westland Wessex. Some military variants were operated in the clear-weather SAR role, with a rescue hoist on the starboard side of the fuselage above the cabin's large sliding door.

A Sikorsky/Westland S-58 Wessex in Arctic camouflage

Sikorsky S-61N Mk II

Country of origin: USA
First flight: August 1972
Type: medium transport
Crew/accommodation: three, and 28 passengers or freight carried internally
Powerplant: two 1,118kW (1,500shp) General Electric CT58 140-1/2
Dimensions: rotor diameter 18.9m (62ft); length with rotors turning 22.2m (72ft 10in)
Max take-off weight: 9,299kg (20,500lb)
Max speed: 254km/h (158mph) at sea level
Cruising speed: 241km/h (150mph)
Max rate of climb: 395m (1,300ft) per minute
Hovering ceiling: 2,652m (8,700ft)
Operational range: 300km (186 miles)
Payload: 3,626kg (7,990lb)
History: built by Sikorsky, plus three hundred, and best known in its Sea King naval form. It was also produced for twenty years in two civil variants, the S-61L and S-61N. The S-61L, capable of carrying 28 passengers, first flew in December 1960, and has fixed tailwheel landing gear. The S-61N is an amphibious type, retaining the Sea King's stabilizing side sponsors with retractable main wheel units. The S-61N Mk II upgrade has accommodation for 26; the AS-61N1, produced by Agusta, is a 24-passenger upgrade with greater range. The civil variant was in production at Sikorsky for 18 years, until 1980.

144 *An S-61N makes a platform landing*

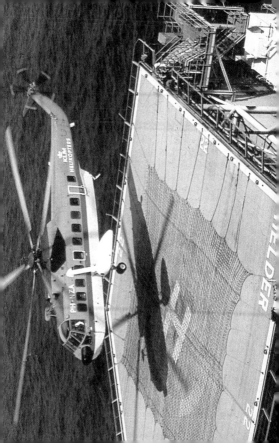

Sikorsky S-61/SH-3H Sea King

Country of origin: USA
First flight: March 1959
Type: multi-role
Crew/accommodation: three crew
Powerplant: two 1,044kW (1,400shp)
General Electric T58-GE-10 turboshafts
Dimensions: rotor diameter 18.9m (62ft);
fuselage length 16.69m (54ft 9in)
Max take-off weight: 9,526kg (21,000lb)
Cruising speed: 219km/h (136mph)
Operational range: 1,006km (625 miles)
Armament: up to 381kg (840lb); this can
include one Mk 44 or Mk 46 homing torpedo,
plus depth charges and anti-ship missiles
Avionics: Canadian Marconi LN-66 radar,
Bendix ASQ-13B or 18 dunking sonar,
sonobuoys, towed MAD and radar warning
History: developed in the late 1950s as a
turboshaft- powered helicopter to act as combined submarine hunter/killer. The S-61 began
life as the HSS-2 with a boat hull, comprehensive electronics and retractable landing gear,
entering service in 1961. Redesignated SH-3A
in 1962, with 932kW (1,250shp) T58-GE-8B
engines, it was developed as the SH-3D, with
T-58-GE-10 engines. Conversions of earlier Sea
Kings supplied the SH-3G utility and the SH-3H
anti-submarine, anti-ship and missile detection.

An SH-3H Sea King off the carrier
Eisenhower

Sikorsky S-61/HH-3E

Country of origin: USA
First flight: 1957 as S-61; 1963 as HH-3
Type: combat search and rescue
Crew/accommodation: three/four crew
Powerplant: two 1,118kW (1,500shp) General Electric T58-GE-5 turboshafts
Dimensions: rotor diameter 18.9m (62ft); length with rotors turning 22.25m (73ft)
Max take-off weight: 10,002kg (22,050lb)
Max speed: 260km/h (162mph) at sea level
Max rate of climb: 671m (2,200ft) per minute
Operational range: 748km (465 miles)
Payload: 25 survivors or 15 litters plus two attendants or up to 2,268kg (5,000lb) of freight
Armament: two 7.62mm (0.3in) Miniguns
History: a few SH-3As for US Navy trials were converted as HH-3As, with more power and fuel, a high-speed hoist, armor and weapons. The US Air Force took over, combined the airframe of the CH-3E with the equipment and weapons of the HH-3A, and produced the HH-3E Jolly Green Giant. A retractable inflight refuelling probe, self-sealing fuel tanks and specialist electronics including an advanced navigation system and sensors were also added. The HH-3F Pelican is operated unarmed by the US Coast Guard, and a similar ASH-3F is built in Italy by Agusta.

The US Coast Guard's highly-developed SAR HH-3F

Sikorsky S-65/CH-53D Sea Stallion

Country of origin: USA
First flight: October 1964
Type: assault and logistics
Crew/accommodation: three, and 55 troops
Powerplant: two 2,027kW (3,025shp) General Electric T64-GE-413 turboshafts
Dimensions: rotor diameter 22.02m (72ft 3in); length with rotors turning 26.9m (88ft 3in)
Max take-off weight: 19,051kg (42,000lb)
Max speed: 315km/h (195mph)
Cruising speed: 278km/h (173mph)
Max rate of climb: 664m (2,180ft) per minute
Operational range: 414km (257 miles)
History: designed as a US Marines helicopter that could fly day or night in adverse weather conditions, load through a ramp-accessed hold small vehicles and artillery, with a sealed fuselage for water landings. Sikorsky used the six-blade rotor and transmission of the CH-54 Tarhe flying crane with a new powerplant and a water tight hull, stabilized by two lateral sponsons holding the retracted main landing gear units. The first delivery of a CH-54A had provision for only 38 troops. Deliveries ended in January 1972, after 265 examples of the CH-53 had been produced.

A CH-53D Sea Stallion upgraded variant of the first production T64-GF-6-powered CH-53A

Sikorsky S-65/MH-53H Super Jolly

Country of origin: USA
First flight: October 1964
Type: combat search and rescue
Crew/accommodation: three or four crew
Powerplant: two 2,927kW (3,925shp) General Electric T64-GE-413 turboshafts
Dimensions: rotor diameter 22.02m (72ft 3in); length with rotors turning 26.9m (88ft 3in)
Max take-off weight: 19,051kg (42,000lb)
Max speed: 315km/h (196mph) at sea level
Operational range: 414km (257 miles)
Armament: two or three 7.62mm (0.3in) Miniguns
Payload: 38 survivors or troops or 24 litters plus attendants or up to 9,091kg (9,000lb) of freight
Avionics: communications, navaids, lighting and advanced flight-control systems to fly missions in 24-hour visual conditions and passive receivers
History: undoubtedly one of the West's most important heavy lift/assault helicopters, and developed into an awesome array of variants. The MH-53H combat SAR/special forces version is based on the HH-53C combat SAR but with improved navigational systems and an infra-red sensor.

A CH-53E, one of the S-65 family, taking on troops in the snow-covered wastes of Norway

Sikorsky S-65/MH-53E Sea Dragon

Country of origin: USA
First flight: 1972 as RH-53D
Type: minesweeping
Crew/accommodation: five seats
Powerplant: three 3,200kW (4,380shp) General Electric T64-GE-416 turboshafts
Dimensions: rotor diameter 24.08m (79ft); length with rotors turning 30.19m (99ft 0.5in)
Max take-off weight: 33,339kg (73,500lb)
Cruising speed: 278km/h (173mph) at sea level
Operational range: 2,075km (1,290 miles)
Avionics: Mk 103 mechanical, Mk 104 acoustic, Mk 105 magnetic and Mk 106 magnetic/acoustic sweeps, plus OEU + Magnetic Orange Pipe for use against shallow-water magnetic mines; night vision equipment, together with other enhanced operational features
History: trials began with the RH-53A conversions from CH-53As which were powered by two T64-GE-413 turboshafts. These have been upgraded considerably in the minesweeping role, to produce the MH-53E Super Stallion and Sea Dragon, using three turboshafts driving improved rotors.

An MH-53E Sea Dragon minesweeping helicopter with a seven-blade main rotor set and canted tailboom

Sikorsky S-70/HH-60A Night Hawk

Country of origin: USA
First flight: October 1974
Type: combat search and rescue
Crew/accommodation: three crew
Powerplant: two 1,260kW (1,690shp) General Electric T700-GE-401 turboshafts
Dimensions: rotor diameter 16.36m (53ft 8in); length with rotors turning 19.76m (64ft 10in)
Max take-off weight: 9,979kg (22,000lb)
Max speed: 269km/h (167mph) at sea level
Operational range: 1,158km (720 miles)
Armament: two 7.62mm (0.3in) machine guns
Payload: 12 survivors or six litters or four litters and three seated survivors or up to 3,629kg (8,000lb) of freight
History. Based on the SH-60B Seahawk, the HH-60A uses the same dynamic system, rescue hoist, radar, FLIR and inertial navigation system. There are now many variants, which include the HH-60H Rescue Hawk combat SAR version developed for the US Navy and based on the SH-60F Seahawk, the HH-60J Seahawk SAR type for the US Marine Corps, which is based on the HH-60H but lacks combat features, and the MH-60K Black Hawk.

The Night Hawk combat rescue version for the USAF had many derivatives, including the US Naval Air Rescue's HH-60H

Sikorsky S-70/UH-60A Black Hawk

Country of origin: USA
First flight: October 1974
Type: light assault transport
Crew/accommodation: three crew
Powerplant: two 1,151kW (1,560shp) General Electric T700-GE-700 turboshafts
Dimensions: rotor diameter 16.36m (53ft 8in); fuselage length 12.6m (41ft 4in)
Max take-off weight: 9,185kg (20,250lb)
Max speed: 296km/h (184mph)
Operational range: 600km (373 miles)
Payload: 14 troops or six litters plus three seats or 3,629kg (8,000lb) external slung load
Armament: General Electric Black Hawk Weapons System – two 7.62mm (0.3in) Miniguns or two pintle-mounted GECAL 150 Gatlings
History: built for the US Army to replace the UH-1Hs, now being refurbished, the S-70 family provides military, naval and commercial helicopters in the 10-tonne (22,050lb) class. The design blends new technology with proven helicopter construction. Entering service in 1979, the sole tactical model is the UH-60A with large sliding side doors, able to carry an infantry squad with rapid ingress/egress in the battlefield.

Born of the Vietnam war, the 1,000th Black Hawk was delivered to the US Army in October 1988

Sikorsky S-70L/SH-60B Seahawk

Country of origin: USA
First flight: December 1979
Type: multi-role shipboard
Crew/accommodation: three crew
Powerplant: two 1,262kW (1,690shp) General Electric T700-GE-401 turboshafts
Dimensions: rotor diameter 16.36m (53ft 8in); length with rotors turning 19.76m (64ft 10in)
Max weight: 9,927kg (21,884lb)
Cruising speed: 249km/h (155mph)
Max rate of climb: 363m (1,192ft) per minute
Armament: two Mk 46 torpedoes
Payload: 3,717kg (8,196lb)
Avionics: Texas Instruments APS-124 radar with fast scanning digital scan converter for link to open integration.
History: using the basic Army UH-60A air frame, the SH-60B Seahawk is a more complicated helicopter; bigger than most others, it was designed to operate from major US surface combatants in both anti-submarine and anti-ship surveillance and targeting missions.

A unique top view of the SH-60B, which as the S-70L won the US Navy's Light Airborne Multi-Purpose System Mk III (LAMPS III) helicopter competition. It has since been ordered in other specialist versions by the US Navy, and for export

Sikorsky H-76 Eagle

Country of origin: USA
First flight: March 1977 as S-76, February 1985 as H-76 prototype
Type: multi-role armed utility
Crew/accommodation: two crew, ten armed troops
Powerplant: two 716kW (960shp) Pratt & Whitney Canada PT6B-36
Dimensions: rotor diameter 13.41m (44ft); length with rotors turning 16m (52ft 6in); fuselage length 13.22m (43ft 4.5in)
Max weight: 4,672kg (10,300lb)
Max speed: 286km/h (178mph)
Max rate of climb: 518m (1,700ft) per minute
Hovering ceiling: 2,652m (8,700ft)
Operational range: 539km (335 miles)
Armament: 7.62mm (0.3in) machine gun, pintle-mounted in each doorway
Payload: 2,127kg (4,690lb)
History: developed as the civil S-76, which became one of the best-selling 12-seat helicopters. Sikorsky decided to proceed with the H-76 and H-76N multi-role naval helicopter without US military procurements. There is an engine option with 548kW (735shp) Allison 250-C34 turboshafts also offered. The H-76 is designed for troop transport and assault, armed escort, anti-armor, search and rescue and air-ambulance.

Sikorsky's light utility military S-76 variant

Sikorsky S-76 Mk II Spirit

Country of origin: USA
First flight: March 1977
Type: light/medium general purpose and transport
Crew/accommodation: two, and 12 passengers
Powerplant: two 600kW (682shp) Allison 250-C30S turboshafts
Dimensions: rotor diameter 13.41m (44ft); length with rotors turning 16m (52ft 6in)
Max take-off weight: 4,672kg (10,300lb)
Cruising speed: 286km/h (178mph) at optimum altitude
Hovering ceiling: 4,875m (16,000ft)
Operational range: 748km (465 miles), with 12 passengers
Payload: up to 1,014kg (4,000lb) slung load
History: developed to increase Sikorsky's share of the corporate/civil market, the S-76 produced excellent performances, capturing 12 records for speed, rate-of-climb and sustained altitude. It is aerodynamically refined and based on the rotor system of the S-70 (UH-60 Black Hawk) military helicopter. Certificated for flight in IFR conditions, it can be arranged for a wide variety of applications. Deliveries of the Mk II began in 1982 with over 40 improvements, including better ventilation and dynamic systems and uprated turboshafts.

Sikorsky S-80/CH-53E Super Stallion

Country of origin: USA
First flight: March 1984
Type: heavy transport
Crew/accommodation: two/three, and 55 troops
Powerplant: three 3,200kW (4,380shp) General Electric T64-GE-416 turboshafts
Dimensions: rotor diameter 24.08m (79ft); length with rotors turning 30.19m (99ft 0.6in); height 8.66m (28ft 5in)
Max take-off weight: 31,639kg (69,750lb)
Max speed: 315km/h (196mph)
Cruising speed: 278km/h (173mph)
Max rate of climb: 762m (2,500ft) per minute
Hovering ceiling: 2,896m (9,500ft)
Operational range: 2,070km (1,290 miles)
Payload: 16,330kg (36,000lb) slung load
History: developed from 1971 to provide an 'urgent' need for an increased assault-transport and heavy lift capability for the Vietnam war; funding was difficult and it was 1984 before the first flight took place. The seven main rotor blades are similar to those of the CH-53, to which the 53E is a lookalike, but they are attached via extension straps which increase the rotor diameter. There is also an MH-53-MCM (mine countermeasures) version with very large sponsons.

The CH-53E has in-flight refuelling capabilities

Wallis WA 116F

Country of origin: UK
First flight: August 1961, as the WA 116
Type: autogyro
Crew/accommodation: two seats in tandem
Powerplant: one 44kW (60hp) Franklin 2A-120 B
Dimensions: rotor diameter 6.1m (20ft 2in); fuselage length 3.4m (11ft 1in)
Max take-off weight: 317.5kg (700lb)
Max speed: 193.6km/h (120.3mph)
Cruising speed: 161km/h (100mph)
Max rate of climb: 305m (1,000ft) per minute
Operational range: 1,300km (808 miles)
History: the WA 116 was the original Wallis design, of which ten were built. One of these was used in the James Bond movie, *You only live twice*. The 116F, detailed above, currently holds nine world rotorcraft records, including speed, range and endurance records for its class. The 116T, which is a dismantled and rebuilt WA 116, first flew in April 1969 and has been used for experimentation on slow flight and short take-off and landing capability, and additionally for electrostatically-charged spraying tests. In 1985, the WA 116/X was developed for all-day and all-night reconnaissance, with a variety of engines.

The WA 120, basically a 116 with a 130hp Rolls-Royce engine and four 70mm (2.76in) aerial cameras

Westland Lynx AH.Mk 1

Country of origin: UK
First flight: March 1971
Type: anti-tank and light assault transport
Crew/accommodation: three crew
Powerplant: two 559kW (750shp) Rolls-Royce Gem 2
Dimensions: rotor diameter 12.8m (42ft); length with rotors turning 15.2m (49ft 9in)
Max take-off weight: 4,536kg (10,000lb)
Cruising speed: 259km/h (161mph)
Operational range: 540km (336 miles)
Payload: 10 troops or 907kg (2,000lb) of freight carried internally, or 1,361kg (3,000lb) of externally-carried freight
History: developed simultaneously for both Army and Navy requirements, the former featured tricycle-wheeled landing gear and the Navy variant twin skids. The Lynx first entered service in 1977 as the AH.Mk 1, since when it has been continually upgraded and diversified. The AH.Mk 1 transport or anti-tank type is equipped with eight TOW missiles. The AH.Mk 7 uses 835kW (1,120shp) Gem 41-1 turboshafts, which provide better hover and maneuver capabilities. The latest variant, the AH.Mk 9 unarmed command post variant with Gem 42-1 turboshafts, features new BERP rotor blades.

Six prototypes were built by Westland, the first of which flew in 1971

170

Westland Lynx HAS.Mk 2

Country of origin: UK
First flight: May 1972
Type: anti-submarine and anti-ship
Crew/accommodation: four seats
Powerplant: two 671kW (900shp) Rolls-Royce Gem 2 turboshafts
Dimensions: rotor diameter 12.8m (42ft), fuselage length 11.92m (39ft 1.3in)
Max take-off weight: 4,536kg (10,000lb)
Cruising speed: 231km/h (144mph) at sea level
Operational range: 592km (368 miles)
Armament: two Mk 44 or Mk 46 or Sting Ray torpedoes, or two depth charges, or four Sea Skua, Penguin or AS.12 anti-ship missiles
Avionics: full night and almost all-weather capability; mission equipment includes surveillance radar, IFF and ESM. Anti-submarine equipment includes towed MAD, dipping sonar and marine markers.
History: the naval Lynx has a folding tail, and fixed tricycle landing gear. The updated Mk 3 and French Mk 4 versions are powered by 835kW (1,120shp) Gem 41-1 turboshafts. A Racal Control Data system was introduced on the Mk 8, together with a thermal imaging Passive Identification Device and either Sea Spray Mk 3 or MEL Super Searcher radar.

Westland Lynx Mk 3

Country of origin: UK
First flight: March 1971
Type: anti-armor
Crew/accommodation: two crew
Powerplant: two 832kW (1,115shp) Rolls Royce Gem 60 turboshafts
Dimensions: rotor diameter 12.8m (42ft); fuselage length 13.79m (45ft 3in)
Max take-off weight: 5,896kg (13,000lb)
Max speed: 306km/h (190mph)
Operational range: 621km (386 miles)
Armament: one 20mm (0.78in) and one 7.62mm (0.3in) machine gun, plus provision to mount Stinger missiles, Euromissiles HOT, Hughes TOW and Rockwell Hellfire anti-armor missiles
History: the Lynx Mk 3 entered production in 1976 as a dedicated anti-armor helicopter. The Lynx is the only helicopter to have been designed by Westland, and planned as a multi-role military, naval and civil machine in the 4.5-tonne (9,922lb) category. It was part of the Anglo-French Helicopter Agreement of 1967, and 30 per cent of the manufacture was carried out by Aérospatiale. The second generation of Lynx, larger, heavier and more powerful, first flew in 1984.

A Westland Lynx HAS.3, widely exported to South America, Europe
and the Middle East

Westland Sea King HAR.Mk 3

Country of origin: UK/USA
First flight: September 1967 from USA-supplied components
Type: search and rescue
Crew/accommodation: four crew
Powerplant: two 1,238kW (1,660shp) Rolls Royce (Bristol Siddeley) Gnome H.1400-1 turboshafts
Dimensions: rotor diameter 18.9m (62ft); length with rotors turning 22.15m (72ft 8in)
Max take-off weight: 9,525kg (21,000lb)
Max speed: 207km/h (129mph) at sea level
Operational range: 1,230km (765 miles)
Payload: 19 survivors, or six litters, or two litters with eleven seated survivors, or up to 2,722kg (6,000lb) freight
Avionics: all-weather flight instrumentation, stability-augmentation system, advanced navigation system, MEL search radar
History: the British license-built version of the Sikorsky S 61 has a 272kg (600lb) capacity rescue hoist, in the SH-3 version supplied to the US Navy, which is identical to that of both the Agusta and Mitsubishi export production helicopters. The HAR.Mk 3 is regarded as the most capable of the search and rescue versions, the last of which was delivered in 1979.

An RAF Sea King HAR.Mk 3 rescue helicopter at RAF Greenham Common in 1981

Westland Sea King HC.Mk 4

Country of origin: UK/USA
First flight: September 1973
Type: assault transport
Crew/accommodation: two or three crew
Powerplant: two 1,238kW (1,660shp) Rolls-Royce Gnome H.1400-1 turboshafts
Dimensions: rotor diameter 18.9m (62ft); fuselage length 17.01m (55ft 9.75in)
Max take-off weight: 9,526kg (21,000lb)
Cruising speed: 207km/h (129mph)
Operational range: 444km (276 miles)
Armament: two 7.62mm (0.3in) machine guns
Payload: 27 troops in amphibious assault role or 2,722kg (6,000lb) of freight carried internally, or 3,400kg (7,500lb) slung load
History: the Sea King assault transport variant HC.Mk 4 was supplied to the Royal Marines in 1979, as its commando version tactical helicopter. It featured non-retracting tailwheel landing gear and no sponsors. The Commando Mk 1 and improved Mk 2 are export variants. Today, all Sea Kings are fitted with composite main-rotor blades produced by computer-controlled filament winding and tankage arranged in two wholly separate systems, plus an optional additional underfloor tank which raises capacity to 3,719 litres (818Imp gal/983US gal).

Westland Sea King HAS.Mk 5

Country of origin: UK/USA
First flight: May 1969
Type: anti-submarine
Crew/accommodation: four seats
Powerplant: two 1,238kW (1,660shp) Rolls-Royce Gnome H.1400-1 turboshafts
Dimensions: rotor diameter 10.0m (62ft) length with rotors turning 22.15m (72ft 8in)
Weight: 6,202kg (13,672lb) empty
Max speed: 230km/h (143mph)
Max rate of climb: 616m (2,020ft) per minute
Hovering ceiling: 975m (3,200ft)
Operational range: 1,230km (764 miles)
Armament: four Mk 46 or Sting Ray torpedoes or four depth charges
Avionics: Ekco AW391 radar, HAS.Mk 5 with MEL Sea Searcher radar, plus Plessey 195 dunking sonar, sonobuoys, advanced LAPADS acoustic processing system, and Racal MIR-2 Orange Crop ESM
History: the Westland-built British equivalent of the SH-3, but with improved electronics. Other variants, apart from those mentioned in earlier pages, include the AEW.Mk 2 with Searchwater early-warning radar. Improvements to the HAS.Mk 6 include greater power, composite main rotor blades, and electronic and armament upgrades, including Sea Eagle anti-ship missiles

180 *An SH-3 with British electronics*

Westland Wasp HAS.1

Country of origin: UK
First flight: July 1958
Type: anti-submarine warfare
Crew/accommodation: two crew
Powerplant: one 529kW (710shp) Rolls-Royce Nimbus 503
Dimensions: rotor diameter 9.83m (32ft 3in); length with rotors turning 12.29m (40ft 4in)
Weight: 1,579kg (3,480lb) empty
Max speed: 193km/h (120mph)
Max rate of climb: 439m (1,440ft) per minute
Operational range: 435km (270 miles)
Armament: intended to drop torpedoes at a point directed by the parent ship, but this altered to general missile attack with the front observer trained to guide SS.11 or AS.12 missiles
Avionics: blind flying instruments and full night equipment
History: both the naval Wasp and the Scout multi-role tactical army version were original designs of Saunders-Roe Company in 1957. Saro took over, and completed the first flight. In 1959, the Nimbus turbo engine was added and the Scout AH.1 first flew in August 1960, and the Wasp HAS.1 in October 1962. Saro was itself taken over by Westland in 1960, and 258 units produced, including export variants for South Africa, Brazil, the Netherlands and New Zealand.

Westland Wessex HC.Mk 2

Country of origin: UK/USA
First flight: May 1957
Type: tactical transport and general purpose
Crew/accommodation: three crew
Powerplant: two 1,007kW (1,350shp) Rolls-Royce (Bristol Siddeley) Gnome H.1000 Mk 110/111 turboshafts
Dimensions: rotor diameter 17.1m (56ft); length with rotors turning 24.04m (65ft 9in)
Max take-off weight: 6,123kg (13,500lb)
Max speed: 212km/h (132mph) at sea level
Cruising speed: 195km/h (121mph)
Operational range: 769km (478 miles)
Payload: 16 troops or 1,814kg (4,000lb) slung load
Avionics: duplicated flight control, day/night and adverse weather capability, overwater navigation and auto-approach to hover for dipping sonar operations
History: a Sikorsky S-58 built under license by Westland, but with the power provided by Rolls-Royce turboshafts, combining the submarine hunter and submarine killer roles. The original Mk 1s were fitted with a single 1,081kW (1,450shp) Gazelle free-turbine; these were later upgraded and became Mk 3s. The Mk 2s began to enter service in February 1964, and two Mk 4 VIP versions were produced for the Queen's Flight.

A Westland Wessex demonstrates its lifting capabilities

Westland Whirlwind HAR.Mk 10

Country of origin: UK/USA
First flight: November 1952 as the Sikorsky S-55
Type: tactical transport and search and rescue
Crew/accommodation: three, and eight troops
Powerplant: one 783kW (1,050shp) Rolls-Royce (Bristol Siddeley) Gnome H.1000 turboshaft
Dimensions: rotor diameter 16.15m (53ft); fuselage length 13.46m (44ft 2in)
Max take-off weight: 3,629kg (8,000lb)
Max speed: 167km/h (104mph)
Operational range: 482km (300 miles)
Armament: four AS.11 anti-tank missiles or two 7.62mm (0.3in) machine guns
History: a license-built version of the Sikorsky S-55, but with turboshaft power, which produced a much-improved helicopter. About 60 of the original HAR.Mk 2 variant were built for SAR and communications roles — these were powered by the 447kW (600hp) Pratt & Whitney engines. Mk 4s were equipped for hot-and-high operations. Original turbo power was provided by General Electric T58s, later built in the UK under license, resulting in the vastly more capable HAR.Mk 10 for the RAF. A refitting program was also carried out to modify the older machines to the Mk 10 standard.

The Mk 10 provides greater payload

Westland (Bristol) Belvedere HC.Mk 1

Country of origin: UK
First flight: January 1952 as experimental Type 173
Type: tactical transport
Crew/accommodation: two or three, and 18 troops or 12 casualties
Powerplant: two 1,230kW (1,650shp) Napier Gazelle NGa.2 Mk 101
Dimensions: rotor diameter (both) 14.91m (48ft 11in); fuselage length 16.56m (54ft 4in)
Max take-off weight: 9,072kg (20,000lb)
Max speed: 222km/h (138mph) at sea level
Operational range: 716km (445 miles)
Armament: none
Payload: up to 2,722kg (6,000lb) internally-carried freight or 2,381kg (5,250lb) externally
History: the RAF's first twin-engined, twin-rotor helicopter began life as the Type 173, which was later developed into the Type 192, which was the basis for the Belvedere HC.Mk 1 all-purpose transport helicopter. A large loading door is sited on the starboard side of the fuselage. There is twin-unit landing gear. Either of the turboshaft engines is capable of driving both rotors in the event of an emergency. Deliveries ceased in June 1962, after only 24 units had been delivered.

The Belvedere saw service in Africa and Asia

188

Westland (Fairey) Rotodyne

Country of origin: UK
First flight: 1947 as Gyrodyne
Type: hybrid helicopter/airplane transport
Crew/accommodation: two, and 40 passengers
Powerplant: two 2,237kW (3,000shp) Napier Eland NE1.3
Dimensions: rotor diameter 27.43m (90ft); fuselage length 17.88m (58ft 8in)
Max take-off weight: 17,237kg (38,000lb)
Max speed: 297km/h (185mph)
Operational range: 724km (450 miles)
History: this hybrid type originated with the Gyrodyne helicopter of 1947, which was powered by an Alvis Leonides radial engine, driving both a rotor and two tractor propellers sited at the tip of each stub wing. This was followed by a Jet Gyrodyne, with a two-blade rotor and tip-mounted pressure jets fuelled by kerosene mixed and burned with air, supplied from a compressor mounted on the fuselage. In addition, there were pusher engines at each wingtip, to avoid torque. In 1953, a 40-seat Rotodyne was ordered which first flew in 1957. After considerable testing in helicopter mode, wingborne flights began in April 1958. Westland bought Fairey in 1960, but its proposal for a 75-seat transport Rotodyne 2 helicopter for the RAF was cancelled in 1962.

Abbreviations

cu ft: cubic feet
ft: feet
gal: gallon
hp: horsepower
Imp gal: Imperial gallon
in: inches
km: kilometres
km/h: kilometres per hour
kW: kilowatt
lb: pounds
m: metres
m³: cubic metres
max: maximum
Mk: Mark
mm: millimetres
min: minute
mph: miles per hour
SAR: search and rescue
sec: second
shp: shaft horsepower
™: Trademark